Customer Liaison

IT Infrastructure Library

Neville Greenhalgh
Melanie Smaridge
(PA Consultancy)

Gildengate House,
Upper Green Lane,
Norwich, NR3 1DW

© Copyright: Controller of HMSO, 1990

First published: 1990

ISBN: 0 11 330546 X

This is one of the books in the IT Infrastructure Library series. At regular intervals, further books will be published and the Library will be completed by late 1991. Since many customers would like to receive the IT Infrastructure Library books automatically on publication, a standing order service has been set up. For further details on standing orders please contact:

HMSO Publicity(P9D), FREEPOST,
Norwich, NR3 1BR
(*No stamp needed for UK customers*).

Until the whole Library is published, and subject to availability, draft copies of unpublished books may be obtained from CCTA if you are a standing order customer. To obtain drafts please contact:

IT Infrastructure Management Services,
CCTA, Gildengate House,
Upper Green Lane,
Norwich, NR3 1DW.

For further information on other CCTA products, contact:

Press and Public Relations,
CCTA,
Riverwalk House,
157-161 Millbank,
London, SW1P 4RT.

This document has been produced using procedures conforming to
BSI 5750 Part 1: 1987; ISO 9001: 1987.

Table of contents

Foreword

Welcome to the IT Infrastructure Library module on **Customer Liaison.**

In their respective subject areas, the IT Infrastructure Library publications complement and provide more detail than the IS Guides.

The ethos behind the development of the IT Infrastructure Library is the recognition that organizations are becoming increasingly dependent on IT in order to satisfy their corporate aims and meet their business needs. This growing dependency leads to a growing requirement for high-quality IT services. In this context quality means matched to business needs and user requirements as these evolve.

This module is one of a series of codes of practice intended to facilitate the quality management of IT services, and of the IT infrastructure. (By IT infrastructure, we mean organizations' computers and networks - hardware, software and computer-related telecommunications, upon which applications systems and IT services are built and run). The codes of practice are intended to assist organizations to provide quality IT service in the face of skill shortages, system complexity, rapid change, current and future user requirements, growing user expectations, etc.

Underpinning the IT infrastructure is the environmental infrastructure upon which it is built. Environmental topics are covered in separate sets of guides within the IT Infrastructure Library.

IT infrastructure management is a complex subject which for presentational and practical reasons has been broken down within the IT Infrastructure Library into a series of modules. A complete list of current and planned modules is available from the CCTA IT Infrastructure Management Services at the address given at the back of this module.

The structure of this module is in essence:

* a Management summary aimed at senior IT managers (Directors of IT and above) and some 'senior customers'; (typically Civil Service grades 3 to 7)

* the main body of the text aimed at IT middle management (typically grades 7 to HEO).

The module gives the main **guidance** in sections 3 to 5; explains the **benefits, costs and possible problems** in section 6, which may be of interest to senior staff; and provides information on **tools** (requirements and examples of real-life availability) in section 7.

CCTA is working with the IT industry to foster the development of software tools to underpin the guidance contained within the codes of practice (ie to make adherence to the module more practicable), and ultimately to automate functions.

If you have any comments on this or other modules, do please let us know. A comment sheet is provided with every module; please feel free to photocopy the comment sheet or to let us have your views via any other medium.

Thank you. We hope you find this module useful.

Acknowledgement

The assistance of Melanie Smaridge (under contract to CCTA from PA Consultancy) is gratefully acknowledged.

1. Management summary

Organizations are becoming increasingly dependent on IT to meet their corporate aims and business needs. It is essential that IT Services (the group responsible for providing IT services):

* provide the right quality of services to meet their customers' requirements

* help their customers to make the best use of these services

* are receptive to their customers' needs and problems and provide them with effective support at all times.

To achieve these objectives requires effective customer liaison - communication and co-operation between IT Services and their customers, and commitment from both parties to a good working relationship.

Organizations need to evaluate their existing liaison activities and procedures and identify improvements needed. This module provides guidance on how IT Services should plan, implement and manage effective customer liaison.

The IT Services Manager has overall responsibility for customer liaison by IT Services. Whilst the guidance in this module is directed at IT Services management, much of the advice is generic and can be used across the IT Directorate as a whole.

All IT Services staff have a part to play in effective customer liaison. However, staff with specific customer liaison responsibilities are needed to manage ongoing customer support, and any particular liaison initiatives which the organization wishes to undertake.

The need to commit IT Services' resources to customer liaison does not necessarily mean appointing a Customer Liaison Manager with that as his or her sole responsibility. In many organizations responsibility can be allocated to one or more IT managers such as the Service Level Manager or Help Desk Manager. If, however, specific liaison responsibilities are allocated to different managers, it is important that their responsibilities are clearly defined and managed.

Ongoing customer liaison is an extension of many of the IT infrastructure management functions which are covered by the IT Infrastructure Library. The relationship between this module and the other modules in the Library is covered in some detail in the introduction (see 2.4).

IT Services need to be continually conscious of their customers' perception of the services being provided. This module explains the need for a professional approach to all contacts with customers, to provide the right working environment for customers to make effective use of IT services.

Customer liaison initiatives should be undertaken where necessary to improve customer relations, and guidance is provided on how to plan and manage different types of initiatives such as a customer satisfaction survey and a customer care programme. The IT Services Manager should establish clear objectives for any initiatives and must involve senior customer management.

Customers have a responsibility to define what IT services they require but cannot be expected to have extensive knowledge of the costs and practicalities of providing these services. One function of customer liaison staff is to bridge this knowledge gap, and provide an effective interface between IT service providers and their customers.

Effective customer liaison will, in the long-term, enable organizations to achieve a better return on IT investment through the more effective use of IT by customers. It will also reduce IT costs in dealing with customer queries and complaints. Organizations should adopt a management policy for customer liaison as part of their overall IS strategy.

Implementing the guidance in this module will help IT Services to develop a co-operative partnership with their customers to their mutual benefit.

2. Introduction

2.1 Purpose

The purpose of this module of the IT Infrastructure Library is to provide guidance on how to plan, implement and manage effective liaison between the providers of IT services and the customers of these services, and to explain the importance of effective liaison in the provision of quality IT services.

2.2 Target readership

This module is aimed at IT Services Managers, Customer Liaison/User Liaison Managers, Service Level Managers, Help Desk Managers and Change Managers and other IT staff with customer liaison responsibilities. The module will also be of interest to Customer/Business Managers.

2.3 Scope

2.3.1 Quality IT services and customer service

An IT Services Manager should aim to provide quality IT services, with the resources available. Quality is determined by fitness for purpose, and quality IT services are those which consistently meet business needs and customer requirements. Effective liaison between IT service providers and their customers, is an essential aspect of the provision of quality IT services. IT service providers must understand the purposes to which IT services are put, and provide services that fit these purposes.

Users of IT services are the customers of the IT Services section. Whether or not they are being charged for IT services, they should be treated as customers, and their views taken into account. The IT service providers must continuously seek to improve their standard of service to customers. IT Services must research and respond to customers' views and effectively and efficiently support their customers' use of IT services.

This module gives guidance to organizations on how to plan, implement and operate effective customer liaison. It concentrates on the following issues:

* customer support (section 2.3.2)

* professional customer contacts (section 2.3.3)

* customer liaison initiatives (section 2.3.4).

2.3.2 Customer support

This module explains the need for resources from IT Services to be committed to customer support, and explains how to provide this support to:

* advise and assist IT customers to make the best use of IT services

* ensure that IT service providers are aware of customers' views, and bear them in mind during the planning and provision of services

* enable IT Services and its customers to jointly determine (in line with overall IS strategies and IT strategic and tactical plans) future requirements for IT services, so as to derive maximum benefit for the organization as a whole.

2.3.3 Professional customer contacts

IT Services Managers need to be concerned about customer perceptions of IT Services. This module explains the importance of IT Services conducting their contacts with customers professionally - in an efficient, honest and courteous manner - and covers the procedure required to ensure that contacts are conducted in this way. A professional approach to customer contact is needed to provide a climate for customers to make effective use of IT services.

2.3.4 Customer liaison initiatives

This module describes initiatives which the IT Services Manager can instigate to improve customer relations, and the procedures required to carry out these initiatives, which are to:

* research customer satisfaction through surveys

* improve IT staff attitudes to customers through a customer care programme

* publicize IT Services to particular groups of customers, and raise awareness of IT in the organization.

2.3.5 Responsibility for customer liaison

Overall responsibility for customer liaison lies with the IT Services Manager. Within a very large organization the IT Services section should dedicate one or more staff, including a full time Customer Liaison Manager, to customer liaison activities. In most organizations however, responsibility for customer liaison is combined with other IT management responsibilities, such as the role of the Service Level Manager or the Help Desk Manager (see 3.3 for examples).

In this module the terms Customer Liaison Manager and customer liaison staff refer to the manager and staff who are given responsibility for customer liaison, whether or not they are full time and whether or not the IT Services Manager has delegated the responsibility. All IT Services staff have a shared responsibility for producing good customer service, for example they must all act professionally in their contacts with customers and must all put customers' interests first. The guidance in this module is relevant to all of them.

Customer liaison staff are responsible for providing customer support (2.3.2) and for undertaking customer liaison initiatives (2.3.4).

Customer liaison staff maintain a watching brief over IT Services contacts with customers (2.3.3), keeping informed, holding regular (perhaps quarterly) meetings with customers to assess customers' perceptions of the services and instigate any required remedial action, but otherwise intervening or taking initiatives only when it is beneficial to do so.

Most day-to-day contact with customers is via the Help Desk. IT Services Managers such as the Service Level Manager have regular contact with customer management concerning their own functional responsibilities, in addition to any specific customer liaison responsibility which they are given. These contacts are described briefly in Annex B and covered in more detail in other modules, as set out in section 2.4.

2.3.6 IT staff as customers

Liaison between the IT Services Section and other IT staff who are users of IT services, is briefly considered in Annex B. The main focus of this module however is on liaison between IT Services and its business customers.

2.3.7 Customers' role in application development

The customers' role in application development is not considered in detail; it is covered by SSADM and PRINCE. Section 3.1.3.2 sets out when IT Services need to liaise with customers during the development of new systems; for example in specifying service levels at the requirements definition stage.

2.4 Related guidance

This module is one of a series that constitute the CCTA IT Infrastructure Library. Although the module can be read in isolation, it is recommended that it is used in conjunction with other modules.

The modules listed in sections 2.4.1 to 2.4.4 provide guidance on IT infrastructure management functions which closely involve the customer. Refer to these for specific advice on the IT Services/customer interface relating to the functions.

2.4.1 Help Desk

A Help Desk provides a day-to-day contact point between customers and IT Services. It is responsible for dealing with customers queries and problems with IT services, for overseeing the restoration of normal service on the customers' behalf following incidents, and for disseminating day-to-day information about changes and service developments to customers.

Effective customer liaison means building relationships with customers, and assisting customers to make the best possible use of IT services available to them. The Help Desk can make an important contribution to effective liaison.

Help Desk and customer liaison staff must work closely together, and both may be part of an overall Customer Services function within IT Services.

2.4.2 Service level management

Service level management is the process of managing the quality of delivered IT service in the face of changing business needs and customer requirements according to a written agreement, the Service Level Agreement, between the customers and IT Services. A Service Level Agreement (SLA) specifies customers' expectations of the IT service, sets out customers' and IT Services' obligations, and forms a common agreed basis for measuring the quality of service provided.

Service level management is the key to establishing a formal customer/supplier relationship between the customer and the IT service provider. Customer liaison staff support customers to plan and manage their SLAs and foster good relationships between IT Services and customers.

Both service level management staff and customer liaison staff may be part of a Customer Services function within IT Services.

2.4.3 Change management

The **Change Management** module advises organizations on how to handle IT infrastructure and service changes effectively and efficiently.

An ability to absorb a high level of change is essential for effective IT service provision in the face of changing business needs and customer requirements. It is important that customers fully understand and use the change management process and customer liaison staff provide customer support over and above that provided by change management personnel.

Both change management staff and customer liaison staff may be part of a Customer Services function within IT Services.

2.4.4 Other relevant guidance

Other IT Infrastructure Library modules include guidance on the interface between IT Services and their customers:

Capacity Management is concerned with the provision and management of IT capacity to ensure required service levels can be achieved. Projections of business volumes and customer requirements provide an important input to capacity plans, and must come from the customer, usually via the Service Level Manager. Customer liaison staff make customers aware of the capacity implications of changing business operations and may arrange to have them evaluated.

Cost Management for IT Services describes the financial management of IT Services, and the costing and pricing of associated services. Whether customers are charged for IT services or merely receive cost information, customer liaison staff must be aware of the cost management systems and be prepared to provide customer support to deal with difficulties. Customer liaison may also suggest introducing new forms of cost management where this will improve relations with customers.

Problem Management is concerned with minimizing the impact of failures of IT services upon the customers, correcting the root causes of these failures, and preventing problems recurring. Where the cause appears to lie with the customer, or where there is a dispute between the customer and IT Services over whether there is really a fault, customer liaison staff may be involved in the resolution of incidents and problems.

The **Management of Local Processors and Terminals** module provides guidance on the plans and controls needed to manage computers and terminals located in customers' premises. Effective liaison between IT Services and their customers who use local processors and terminals is particularly important.

The **Managing Facilities Management** module provides guidance on the plans and controls required to manage a Facilities Management (FM) contract. The module recommends that any organization using an FM provider retains its own IT expertise in the form of a Service Control Team. Whilst the prime responsibility for customer liaison lies with the FM provider, the SCT oversees the ongoing management of FM and monitors the effectiveness of customer liaison between the FM provider and the customers.

In addition, the following modules concerned with environmental issues contain useful advice for customer liaison staff and customer managers:

* **The Office Working Environment and IT**

* **Managing a Quality Working Environment for IT Users**

* **Office Design**

* **Environmental Human Factors**.

Attention to ergonomic issues (vision, concentration, posture and workplace) is a critical factor in the effectiveness of IT Services. Customer liaison staff need to be aware of ergonomic and environmental issues, and ensure that these issues are adequately addressed.

The CCTA IS Guide B1, **The Users' Role in Systems Development**, contains advice on other aspects of customer (user) involvement with IT. The guide describes the users' role in planning, developing and implementing Information Systems, including defining the level of service to be delivered by the systems when in live operation. IT Services must liaise with the users involved in this process and with the IT Applications Development area from the earliest stages.

The CCTA IS Guide C1, **Services Management**, provides guidance on how effective IT service management is necessary to deliver a quality IT service and explains how customer service is seen as one of the main deliverables of IT service management.

2.5 Standards

ISO9001/EN29000/BS5750 - Quality Management and Quality Assurance Standards

The IT Infrastructure Library modules are designed to assist adherents to obtain third-party quality certification to ISO9001. Organizations' IT Directorates may wish to be so certified. CCTA may in future recommend that Facilities Management providers are also certified to ISO 9000 by a third-party certification body. Such third-parties should be accredited by the NACCB, the National Accreditation Council for Certification Bodies.

PRINCE Project Management Methodology

PRINCE is the recommended CCTA standard for project management. Major initiatives concerning liaison with customers, for example customer care programmes, should be planned and implemented as projects using PRINCE.

3. Planning customer liaison

3.1 Procedures

The following sub-sections describe the purpose of customer liaison and the planning of the procedures required for a customer liaison function within an IT Services organization.

3.1.1 Purpose and principles of customer liaison

The first step in implementing a customer liaison function is to understand fully its importance and the principles involved.

Many service industries are increasing their emphasis on customer service, have put a lot of effort into understanding the customer perspective of the services they provide and altered their services accordingly.

IT Services sections need to adopt the same approach if they are to provide quality services. An internal IT Services section may currently be the sole supplier of IT services to its customers who cannot easily switch to another supplier in the short term. In the longer term however, many customers will have the option of replacing internal IT Services by Facilities Management arrangements. IT service providers wishing to retain their customers must not abuse their sole supplier status. They must understand that effective customer liaison is essential in the provision of quality customer care; they must research and respond to customers' views, and effectively and efficiently support their customers' use of IT services.

The IT services provided must meet the customers' needs if the organization as a whole is to obtain the full benefit from its expenditure on IT.

IT staff are often drawn from a technical background that gives them little understanding of the environment in which IT services are used. Customers are responsible for defining their requirements for the services they expect to receive, but cannot be expected to have an extensive knowledge of the practicalities and costs of providing IT services. There is a need to bridge this knowledge gap and provide an effective interface between IT service providers and their customers.

Whilst customers have been involved in the development of new systems, with formal roles for them defined in the PRINCE methodology, their part in the operation of live systems is less well established. However it is the system in operation with which the customer is primarily concerned and from which the benefits are obtained.

A customer liaison function has a three fold purpose:

* to ensure standard procedures and good practices are used in all contacts between IT Services and its customers

* to provide ongoing customer support

* to undertake and manage specific liaison initiatives; for example a customer care programme.

Effective customer liaison depends on the following principles being followed by IT Services staff:

* customers are invariably dealt with professionally

  - staff are always courteous and helpful

  - all meetings and other contacts are conducted in a business-like manner

  - the quality of service is formally documented in Service Level Agreements (SLAs) and non-adherences to SLAs are tackled urgently and seriously

* effective customer support is provided at all times

  - customers are made aware of the full range of IT services offered, and helped to make the best use of them

  - customers are helped to specify their requirements for new services

  - IT services are tailored to meet customer requirements, not the convenience of service providers

  - customers are helped to identify, define, prioritize and evaluate changes in requirements that will improve the service they receive

  - customer problems with IT services are resolved even where the cause lies in the customer area, for example in inadequate training, or an unsuitable environment, or where there is disagreement between the customers and IT Services about whether there really is a problem

- new customers are assisted to familiarize themselves with the services and to start using them

- new services are fully supported

* customer satisfaction is paramount

- customer satisfaction is regularly monitored

- customer complaints are acted on, and customer views taken into account

- customers receive regular feedback on progress in resolving complaints, problems and other enquiries.

The IT Services Manager has overall responsibility for ensuring that these principles are adopted, but day-to-day control lies with the IT Manager(s) responsible for customer liaison.

Effective customer liaison depends on management commitment, on the quality of customer liaison staff, and on the soundness of customer liaison procedures. Good personal relationships between customer liaison personnel and customers are also important, and customer liaison staff must make efforts to understand the motivation and concerns of their customers.

3.1.2 Introducing customer liaison

3.1.2.1 Overview

Before work starts on introducing customer liaison the IT Services Manager must take responsibility or else appoint someone to be responsible, for the planning and implementation of customer liaison as described in 3.1.4.1. This person will probably be responsible subsequently for the ongoing operation of the customer liaison function. See 3.3 for suggested personal qualities and skill levels of customer liaison personnel.

The first stage of introducing a customer liaison function is to determine its overall objectives. First assess the current status of liaison between the IT Services section and their customers in terms of who is involved, and to identify both satisfactory and unsatisfactory aspects.

In the light of these findings, identify and prioritize objectives for improving customer liaison. Reconcile these objectives with available resources to produce a revised set of objectives with targets delivery dates - include short and long-term objectives. This process may have to be iterative - the resources made available will depend on management approval to proceed at the suggested pace.

Agree the objectives, priorities and timescales with senior IT management and key customer managers. Decide the steps to be taken to achieve the objectives. These steps may involve one-off initiatives such as a customer care programme, or the creation of an ongoing customer support function, or the introduction of new procedures for handling customers; some combination of all three approaches may be required. Allocate responsibility for implementing these changes. Agree the organizational structure appropriate for the size of organization and the objectives and timescales set. Two possible structures are given at section 3.3.

Draw up terms of reference for the customer liaison function, to describe its objectives and, in broad terms, how it is to meet them. See Annex F for example terms of reference. Tell all IT Services and customer staff about the customer liaison function and terms of reference. Let these staff know, in outline, how they will be affected.

The role and specific objectives of customer liaison, particularly in the short-term, depend upon the status of an organization. The following sub-sections cover the introduction of customer liaison in three situations:

* for a greenfield installation or one where formal IT infrastructure management functions are not in operation

* for an installation where the basic IT infrastructure management functions are in operation

* where new systems or services are being introduced or new customers are being taken on.

It is often useful if one customer manager is designated as Customer Co-ordinator to provide a first line of contact for IT Services (see Annex B3).

3.1.2.2 Greenfield installation

For the purposes of this section the term greenfield installation includes an existing site without formal IT infrastructure management functions in operation.

For customer liaison to operate effectively, it is important that Help Desk, service level management and change management functions are in place. At a greenfield installation, or one without adequate procedures for them, set up these functions as a priority.

Give the Help Desk the highest priority. From a customer liaison point of view, it has the greatest effect on day-to-day use of IT services. In addition, urgently implement change management when changes are frequent or if changes are, or are expected to be, disruptive. Plan to implement service level management last, after the internal IT Services functions on which it depends are established.

Setting up these functions involves considerable discussions with customers. Make it an objective of the customer liaison function to use this opportunity to establish the foundation for good, long-term customer relationships.

At this stage the other, short-term, objectives of customer liaison are to:

* identify managers in the customer area with whom liaison is needed and start discussions about long-term customer support (see 3.1.3.1)

* introduce as soon as possible procedures to ensure professionalism in customer contacts (see 3.1.3.4) and incorporate them in induction training for all IT Services staff.

Await the implementation of IT infrastructure management functions such as Help Desk, change management and service level management, before planning any significant customer liaison initiatives (see 3.1.4) or tackling longer term objectives.

3.1.2.3 IT infrastructure management already in operation

Where the basic elements of IT infrastructure management are in place, and customers have considerable experience of the IT services they receive, plan to introduce a customer liaison function as soon as possible.

Begin by assessing the current situation. Investigate the current level of customer satisfaction, and identify the strengths and weaknesses of the IT Services organization and the major issues and difficulties affecting the services, from a customer perspective. Review business plans and identify those IT services, both existing and planned, which are crucial to the achievement of business plans. Then focus on these services.

There are a number of ways of determining how customers feel about the services provided. They include:

* reviewing correspondence, minutes, Help Desk enquiry records, reports and published information about IT service quality; for example relevant information from service level reviews, Help Desk logs, Change Advisory Board documentation, and possibly, customer/user group meetings

* conducting discussions about the quality of IT services at customer forums, for example user groups, branch or regional business meetings

* carrying out a customer satisfaction survey as described in section 3.1.4.1

* conducting a series of interviews with both key customers and IT Services personnel, to develop an understanding of how their respective views on the quality of service provided match - ask how they respectively rate

  - the quality of IT services provided in support of business needs

  - the reaction of IT service providers to business changes

  - the track record of IT service providers in dealing with user enquiries, requests and service problems.

Use this information to decide the detailed objectives for customer liaison. An example of a mission statement on which to base the detailed objectives is:

"To ensure that by effective liaison and customer service ethos, IT Services provides its customers with the support necessary for them to use IT services effectively and efficiently, whilst making the most efficient use of IT resources."

Draw up terms of reference to meet the precise objectives defined for customer liaison. Annex F contains an example.

Achieving the broad objective requires that procedures are planned for:

* ongoing customer support activities, to be carried out by customer liaison staff (see 3.1.3.1)

* handling contacts with customers to be followed by all IT Services staff (see 3.1.3.4)

* initiatives to improve customer relations which may involve all IT Services staff, but are managed by customer liaison staff (see 3.1.4).

3.1.2.4 Introducing new systems/ services and taking on new customers

Plan to have customer liaison in place to cover the development and implementation of a new computer system or services, and the take-on of new customers. It is perfectly acceptable to introduce customer liaison initially for only part of the customer base. The guidance in this subsection applies whether IT Services are already operating IT infrastructure management, or are introducing the key elements as new systems, services, or users are brought on-stream.

Customer liaison staff have an important role in representing IT Services, or co-ordinating their involvement, from development through to implementation of a new system or service, and during the take-on of new customers. The objectives of customer liaison are:

* to ensure customer support is provided that will allow the smooth implementation of the new or extended IT services

* to establish a basis for effective long-term liaison with new customers and with users of new systems and services.

Planning the role of customer liaison staff to meet these objectives is covered in 3.1.3.2 and 3.1.3.3.

3.1.2.5 Facilities management

When IT service provision is being contracted out to an FM provider it is important that responsibilities for customer liaison activities are agreed during the negotiations and are clearly defined in the FM contract from the outset. Adding these responsibilities later, can affect the value-for-money offered by the FM proposals.

Three parties are involved in an FM situation:

* users of IT services and their management

* the IT Directorate

* the FM provider.

Prime responsibility for customer liaison lies with the FM provider, especially if the FM provider is supplying a total service and has responsibility for most of the IT infrastructure management functions. However the IT Directorate needs to retain a Service Control Team (SCT) to manage the organization's relationship with the FM supplier and to retain responsibility for IT management activities such as quality audit and overall IT planning and control.

The SCT oversees the provision of managed service and, specifically, monitors the effectiveness of customer liaison between the FM provider and the customers and independently assesses customer satisfaction. The SCT can provide first line support for customers' business queries. The role of the SCT is explained in detail in the IT Infrastructure Library module **Managing Facilities Management**.

Figure 1 illustrates contacts that take place between the IT service providers and the customers in an FM situation. The SCT handles normal management level contacts with the FM provider. Direct day-to-day contact regarding service provision is normally between the 'hands-on' customers and the FM provider.

**Figure 1:
Liaison contacts in
an FM situation**

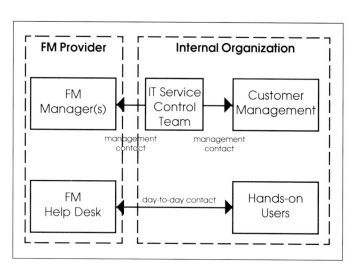

Specify in the contract the respective roles of the FM provider and the SCT and the extent to which ongoing customer support (as described at 3.1.3.1 and 3.1.3.2) is provided by the FM provider.

Professional handling of customer contacts is no less essential in an FM situation than it is where the IT service is provided in-house. The guidance given at 3.1.3.4 applies in either situation.

The SCT in its role of overseeing the ongoing management of FM, monitors the customer care being provided, the professionalism of contacts and the adherence of the FM provider to agreed procedures.

Customer liaison initiatives described in 3.1.4 are undertaken either solely by the FM provider or jointly with the SCT. It is recommended that the FM provider is asked during the procurement to produce a service code of practice which covers the FM providers' customer liaison responsibilities.

3.1.3 Planning for ongoing customer liaison

This sub-section describes the plans needed for the ongoing roles of customer liaison staff:

* providing customer support for existing services/to current users (3.1.3.1)

* providing customer support for new systems or services (3.1.3.2)

* providing customer support for new users (3.1.3.3)

* setting standards for professional customer contacts and overseeing adherence to these standards (3.1.3.4).

Document, review and agree the planned procedures in sufficient detail to make clear to all involved how to carry them out.

3.1.3.1 Customer support for existing services/to current users

Many IT Services staff have some direct contact with customers and they should be as helpful as possible to these customers. However they often do not have the time to provide extensive support to customers. Full or part-time customer liaison staff are needed to provide the right level of support, and for this to be effective they need to acquire a good knowledge of customer businesses.

Where the scale of operations allows, make particular staff responsible for different customer areas. Plan for customer liaison staff who have been given responsibility for customer support, to divide their time between:

* the customer area, with the aim of

    - getting to know the customers' businesses and the ways in which they use IT services

    - building long-term relationships with key customer managers, who must be carefully identified

    - helping customers make best use of the IT services that are available to them

    - assisting customers to understand IT Services procedures

    - helping customers to identify and satisfy requirements for IT training

    - ensuring customers are aware of the effect of IT equipment on their office environment and the ergonomic and environmental issues related to use of their equipment

    - following up calls to the Help Desk which require significant liaison with customers to resolve (for example complaints and vague enquiries)

    - assisting customers to solve problems where the cause appears to be in the customer area; for example because of inadequate training

    - helping customers to identify necessary or desirable improvements to IT services and to express their requirements as requests for change

    - assisting customers to evaluate and consider the impact of changes proposed by IT Services

    - assisting customers to progress major changes that are beyond the authority of the Change Manager/change management system; for example setting up an Information Centre, or a new system procurement

* the IT area, with the aim of

    - achieving professionally handled contacts with customers, and stepping in to resolve problems

    - feeding customer reactions and perspectives to IT Services Managers and staff to keep them informed

    - progressing difficulties identified by customers, which are either not recognized as problems by IT Services or are vague or organizationally awkward

    - helping customers with the procedures for initiating changes or projects to meet their changing requirements

    - assisting where necessary in the resolution of incidents which affect levels of service

    - co-ordinating where necessary the response of different IT Services Managers to customer problems or queries

    - anticipating difficulties that customers might have (including those caused by changes initiated by IT Services) and ensuring that they are avoided.

Document the procedures and responsibilities for these activities and obtain the agreement of senior customer and IT management.

Plan to use these customer support activities as a vehicle for encouraging customers to take an ongoing active part in defining the IT services they require to carry out their businesses.

Obtain the agreement of selected customer managers at senior and middle management level, to act as primary points of contact for customer support. The most likely candidates are customer managers who liaise with the Service Level Manager on Service Level Agreements, or, if available, the managers who acted as User Assurance Co-ordinators during the original development of the various IT systems concerned.

Users of each IT system may be spread across a number of sections/branches or locations, with one customer manager nominated as their representative for the purpose of reviewing service levels.

In this case consider the need to offer customer support to managers in all sections/branches or locations, and for liaison with a wider group of customer managers. Select and obtain the agreement of the managers concerned.

Little of the customer managers' time should be taken up by IT liaison activities, but plan for IT Services to hold regular (say quarterly) meetings with customer managers to review satisfaction and support. Consider whether special meetings are required or whether to cover liaison issues as an extension of Service Level reviews, particularly if the Service Level Manager also has broader customer support responsibilities. Agree a standard agenda for the liaison issues which includes business changes and problems (giving early warning to IT Services), as well as IT difficulties and changes to IT services.

Consider helping the customers to establish user groups. Whilst they should be independent of IT Services, some assistance in setting them up is often given - IT Services may be the only contact between separate groups of customers. Contact between customers, the spread of ideas for better use of IT services and the discussion of common problems can be very helpful to customers.

As a result of their activities, customer liaison staff may recommend IT Services to undertake initiatives to improve customer relations, or to reorganize the provision of IT Services to improve customer service. Plan to give the Customer Liaison Manager(s) a regular item in IT Services management meetings to put forward any recommendations.

Customer support activities do not necessarily need the same amount of effort all the time, but plan for adequate time to be made available when required by customers.

Where relations between IT services providers and customers are poor, it may be difficult to persuade customers to accept customer support from IT Services. Senior customer management must be convinced of the benefits from such support (see Section 6), and they must persuade their staff to co-operate to obtain them.

3.1.3.2 Customer support for new systems or services

Plan for customer liaison staff to provide customer support during the development and implementation of new systems or services, whether for existing or new customers.

The following paragraphs describe the involvement of customer liaison staff at each stage from project initiation through to implementation. The CCTA IS Guide B1, **The Users' role in Systems Development** provides a comprehensive description of all the stages.

Project initiation and feasibility

During the early stages of the development of a new IT system or service the customer is largely concerned with defining the proposed new system or service, with the assistance of IT development staff, and obtaining approval for the system or service. However the potential IT service provider has to liaise with the customer on:

* alternative methods of implementation and acceptance and their feasibility

* cost estimates, especially for running costs

* IT Services' resources required during the development project and beyond.

Plan for customer liaison staff to either fulfil this role or co-ordinate it, to ensure that the potential customers are assisted as much as possible. Discuss the method of implementing and accepting the new system, for example hardware requirements, the extent of parallel running, in sufficient detail to assure both sides that it is feasible. Running cost estimates given at this stage are necessarily tentative, so plan to provide a possible range of costs rather than specific figures. Costs are needed to obtain authorization to proceed.

The IT Services section will have to put resources in to ensure that the project is technically feasible and will not adversely affect existing customers. Post-implementation, IT Services must be resourced to provide ongoing support to customers and to manage what will probably be a larger and more complex portfolio of IT systems and services.

On larger IT projects, managed under PRINCE, there are two formal customer (user) roles:

* the Senior User, who sits on the Project Board, and whose prime responsibility is to represent the interests of all customer departments affected by the project, and to monitor project progress against the requirements of customer management

* the User Assurance Co-ordinator, who sits on the Project Assurance Team, and whose prime responsibility is to ensure all products are of acceptable quality and to represent customer interests on a day-to-day basis.

In addition, customer managers may be appointed as Project Manager or Stage Manager for the IT development project. There are equivalent customer (user) roles for smaller projects, though not always so formally defined.

Customer liaison staff should make direct contact with these key customer managers and make themselves available for advice and clarification of any aspect of the running of IT services.

Specification of the system/service

Perhaps the most important stage in the development of a new IT system or service is the specification stage. The role of customer liaison staff is to ensure both that customers have reasonable expectations of the proposed system or service to be provided, and that IT Services commit themselves to meeting the agreed specification. The project team consists largely of customers and IT development staff but plan for customer liaison staff to liaise with the project team, other IT Services managers and key customers to ensure that:

* the detailed user specification, which includes input and output traffic levels, processing deadlines and volume of data storage required, is technically achievable

* acceptance criteria include operational aspects such as back up facilities, reliability and resilience, as well as processing and response times and volumes of data to be handled

* ergonomic and environmental factors are taken into account in specifying hardware, accommodation and other facilities (such as additional air conditioning or power supplies) required

* estimates of costs are revised, as the system is more precisely defined

* installation plans, which define the approach to be adopted when introducing the system into its operational environment, are complete and realistic and include details of the

- hardware to be installed, including numbers and locations of terminals

- environment required by the hardware, and the people operating it (including an Accommodation Brief drawn up with Office Services)

- conversion or capture of data for testing and live operation of the system

- cutover plan, from existing manual or automated system

- preparations for help facilities, from an IT Services Help Desk and/or customer Help Desk

- fallback options to counter the main risks that may be encountered upon installation

- responsibilities of the customers during installation

(The complexity of the installation plans depends upon the complexity and geographical distribution of the new system. For example distributed systems of terminals and small computers require additional planning - see the IT Infrastructure Library module **Management of Local Processors and Terminals** for further details)

* training required by customer and IT Services staff is identified

* security measures are identified (preferably by using CRAMM)

* relevant technical and operability standards are identified (see the IT Infrastructure Library module on **Computer Operations Management**) and requirements for integration with other systems

* service levels required to achieve the projected benefits are specified (and achievable).

The system specification is signed off by the customers and forms the basis for the development of the system or the IT service(s) to be provided. The IT Services Manager should also sign off the specification, thus demonstrating the commitment of IT Services to meeting it, and their belief in its feasibility.

Procurement

When new or additional equipment has to be procured to implement new systems or services, the project team needs to prepare an Operational Requirement (or other equivalent document), which forms the basis of procurement. IT Services helps the project team to prepare the OR and to evaluate the bids received. Plan for customer liaison staff to provide guidance to the customer to ensure that the following requirements are specified:

* all relevant requirements (including user requirements) from the specification stage

* requirements for training and documentation for use of the proposed system (and for operating it) are specified

* maintenance requirements and support from the suppliers

* operating facilities and systems software required to run the service as specified, including requirements for automated management and operation of the service.

Ensure all factors which influence the service levels and running costs of the final IT service are taken into account in the procurement process. Government organizations should involve their CCTA Procurement Officer as early as possible in procurement projects.

System design and development

The design of the specified IT system is largely carried out by IT development staff in direct consultation with customers. IT Services involvement at this stage is limited to liaison with IT development staff on design aspects which affect the end service to the customer.

The development stage is carried out jointly by IT developers, who write and test the programs and procedures and produce the documentation, and customer staff.

Plan for customer liaison staff to have a co-ordinating role to ensure that the necessary IT facilities are provided for systems development work.

Comprehensive documentation about the new system or services is important for future support and for training customer and IT Services staff before implementation commences. Documentation is the responsibility of the project team including customer staff until implementation, but because of its importance, customer liaison staff need to co-operate with the project team to ensure that all documentation is:

* delivered on time

* accessible to those who need it

* kept up to date.

Documentation is a vital part of the system. Control amendments as part of the project's change management system throughout development and testing, and then under IT Services' change management procedures after implementation. Customer liaison staff need to co-ordinate the handover of documentation at the time of implementation.

Installation, testing and operation

Towards the end of the development stage, IT Services' involvement increases dramatically and the project team includes more IT Services staff. Customer liaison staff have considerable involvement at this time. It is important that they use the opportunity to establish good relationships between IT Services and their customers.

During the installation and acceptance of new equipment, systems, or services customer liaison staff work with customers (end-users and their management), and on their behalf within the IT Directorate, to ensure a smooth and effective implementation process. This collaboration reduces the effort that will be needed later for customer support and remedial action.

Before customer acceptance testing begins, the installation team installs the new system or service. The preparation for customer acceptance testing consists of:

* training all staff, end-user and IT Services, who will be involved in the operation of the new system (Customer liaison arranges for customer training to be provided)

* converting data files or carrying out data entry (largely the responsibility of the development team)

* installing new hardware and software at central computer site(s) and in the customer domain (largely IT Services responsibility - customer liaison staff ensure customers know what to do and in case of difficulties who to contact)

* taking the release package (software, documentation etc) into IT Services control (customer liaison staff inform customers of any actions they must take or of anything that may affect them)

* distributing user manual, maintenance and operational documentation and business procedures for the use of the new system (customer liaison staff act as the main interface with customers).

Customer liaison staff need to maintain regular contact with customer management to check that they are satisfied with the installation activity and to deal with customer problems and queries. It is important for future relationships with customers that the liaison, at this first stage of IT Services' responsibility for the new system or service, is handled well.

The development project continues for a period after acceptance, to ensure the system has settled in satisfactorily. Customer liaison staff need to be involved in the post-implementation review of development projects to identify areas for improved liaison between IT Services and customers both for the current project and for future projects. Any requirement for earlier involvement of IT Services in future projects and for better collaboration between customers and IT Services must be spelt out: it is common for IT Services to be involved far too late in development projects.

Once the new system has been accepted, a formal process involving sign off by the Project Board, customers and IT Services, the Service Level Agreement, if one exists, becomes operative and IT Services take on responsibility for operating the new system. It is likely that increased support will be needed during the first six months of live operation. Customer liaison staff should be allocated to provide extra support resources.

On disbandment of the development project, the formal roles of Senior User and User Assurance Co-ordinator are terminated. However the individuals will have gained valuable knowledge of the IT system and will have negotiated the Service Level Agreement covering this system. If possible, retain their involvement as the key customer staff for liaison with IT Services, and give them responsibilities for:

* reviewing and renewing service level agreements

* signing-off and prioritizing changes to the system

> *   defining customer support required.

This arrangement benefits both customers and IT Services.

3.1.3.3 Customer support to new users of existing services

Where existing services are to be extended to cover other parts of the organization, customer liaison should ensure that:

*   key individuals from the new customer community are appointed to represent that community at senior and middle management levels

*   the new customers are aware of the full range of services on offer and the role and activities of customer liaison

*   the new customers are aware of their own representatives, and are encouraged to raise suggestions for improvement

*   ergonomic and environmental issues are taken into account and adequate accommodation made available for the new customers

*   workable SLAs are negotiated with the new customers' representatives

*   Help Desk and maintenance/installation staff are made aware of the new customers

*   the new customers have the Help Desk number and understand they must report all problems and difficulties which they have to the Help Desk

*   other support needed to help the new customers to learn to use the services is provided

*   the new customers are informed about any relevant user groups

*   the new customers understand how their use of the services will be costed and charged for.

3.1.3.4 Reviews of customer support

Plan to review the effectiveness of customer support activities after say the first six months and then annually. Decide who to involve, how to measure the effectiveness and progress achieved and how to identify the required follow-up actions (see 5.1.2.1).

3.1.3.5 Professional customer contacts

Professional handling of all IT Services contacts with customers is the key to establishing an effective relationship with customers. Professional, in this context, means:

* courteous and polite

    - letting the person know that they matter, rather than giving the impression that they are a nuisance

    - apologizing if a customer appears to have received poor service irrespective of whose fault it was (people can still be sorry that the customer has been inconvenienced, and investigate the cause later)

* honest

    - never promise what cannot be delivered

    - always carry out agreed actions or, if it is not possible, contact the customer again to explain what has not been done and why

* efficient

    - act quickly, and respond to the customer as soon as possible, to let them know where they stand and what actions are being taken as a result of their contact

    - let the customer know their contact has been noted, and is being acted on, even if it cannot be dealt with yet

* helpful

    - if unable to help, pass the customer on to someone who can but never just give another name to get rid of him/her

    - if the necessary contact is unknown promise to find out and get back to the customer within a specified time

* documenting contacts

    - using call report forms, minutes, and the like, inform the relevant managers by providing them with a copy of the documentation; if a customer is unhappy, inform the manager with customer liaison responsibility for that customer

* ensuring that contacts with IT Services are followed through to a satisfactory conclusion from the customer's point of view

    - by the customer's original point of contact within IT Services or, if responsibility has been passed to someone else within IT Services, by them.

Prepare the documentation, embodying these points, of procedures for handling contacts with customers. If procedures covering for example meetings, phone calls, and reports are in operation and documented within other parts of the·organization, use them. Modify them if absolutely necessary. Where procedures do not already exist, write and publish them. Also, plan to review the procedures including how to measure their effectiveness (see 5.1.2.2).

Procedures are not necessarily followed just because they are written down. Time must be planned to explain to IT Services staff the importance of the procedures. Allow time for discussion and review of drafts by all who are obliged to follow them. Ensure staff realize that all contacts that take place between customers and them are covered by the procedures, not only those formal contacts defined in other procedures such as Help Desk scripts.

Annex D provides more detailed guidance on customer contacts and illustrates the type of procedures which should be established and followed. The annex covers:

* meetings

* phone calls

* correspondence

* IT Services publications for example User Manuals, reports etc

* electronic messages

* attendance at customer sites.

Consider at this stage, whether the tools and facilities required to follow the procedures are available and adequate to support them. Have all necessary personnel access to a suitable typing service, or word processor, to produce notes of meetings, and to type correspondence?

Are forms widely available for call reports? If not, plan the introduction or extension of such facilities. Agree standard formats for notes of meetings, call reports, letters, minutes and publications and set them up on staff's word processing systems where relevant.

Expenditure required to provide adequate tools and facilities needs to be cost justified, agreed and budgeted for. The benefits are savings in staff time and improved customer service.

3.1.4 Planning customer liaison initiatives

This sub-section describes the planning of customer liaison initiatives.

Customer liaison staff, as a result of customer support activities, can call for reviews of activities and deliverables which are the responsibility of other IT Services Managers. Such activities and deliverables include:

* capacity plans

* cost management

* service level agreements.

See the IT Infrastructure Library modules referenced in section 2.4 for guidance on reviewing these items.

The planning and implementation of initiatives that are directly concerned with liaison with customers including:

* customer satisfaction surveys

* customer care programmes

* publicity drives

is the responsibility of the Customer Liaison Manager or the IT Services Manager(s) with responsibility for customer liaison.

Manage these initiatives as projects under PRINCE where appropriate and involve senior IT and customer management.

3.1.4.1 Customer satisfaction survey

Break down the planning of a customer satisfaction survey to address the four main stages outlined below:

* defining the objectives of the survey

* designing and planning the survey

* gathering and analysing the answers

* interpreting and reporting.

Stage one: defining the objectives of the survey

When defining the objectives of a survey consider the following questions:

* what is the purpose of the survey?

* what issues should the survey address?

* what is the target readership of the survey report?

* what actions may follow from the results?

* what value is expected to be obtained from the survey?

* what information is already available, for example from service level reviews, complaints and Help Desk calls, problem records, requests for terminals?

* what further information is required and from whom (distinguish between what is essential, and what would be nice to know, and include only the former)?

It is important for the commissioner of the survey to clearly define the objectives. Too often, surveys undertaken without clear objectives produce results that are too vague, too narrow, or just inappropriate.

Phrase the objectives in specific, action-orientated terms for example:

* to identify the major irritants that cause customers to be dissatisfied, or put them off using existing IT services

* to identify ways in which more customers could be persuaded to use existing IT services

* to enhance the performance of the Help Desk, change management or any other aspect of IT Services

* to obtain customer feedback on new and/or modified IT services.

Draw up a concise written statement of the objectives of the survey, including any budgetary or time constraints. Obtain the agreement of the IT Services Manager and the managers of any staff being asked for their opinions. The support of senior customer managers is essential when customers are expected to make time to respond to the survey.

Stage two: designing and planning the survey

Decide at this stage what questions are to be asked, of whom, when, and by whom, and how the answers are to be analyzed.

Decide what type of survey is to be carried out. Use one or more of the following methods:

* written questionnaires, with a large number of questions, some of which may require some thought to answer, covering any number of people selected either specifically or at random (useful for statistical answers, for example x% of customers use a particular service for more than 20 hours a week)

* telephone interviews, asking a large number of people a small number of specific questions (these can be completed very quickly using Help Desk staff)

* interviews in depth with a limited number of key individuals (a deeper understanding of customers' opinions and preferences can be gained from face-to-face interviews using open ended questions)

* group discussions for specific customer groups or to debate specific customer concerns (these can generate realistic improvement ideas, but need very skilled handling).

When choosing the method balance the cost, effort involved, and time and resources available from both the customers' and surveyors' point of view against the expected value of results.

For very large surveys expert assistance (for example from market researchers) may be needed. Remember the need to budget for this.

If a questionnaire is to be used, design it carefully. Questionnaire design is a skilled process. Call upon any specialist expertise in the organization if it exists, otherwise consider the use of outside experts to design complex questionnaires. Guidelines on designing, producing and using questionnaires are provided at Annex C, along with a sample customer satisfaction questionnaire.

Pilot the use of questionnaires where possible. Plan the analysis of results in parallel with the questionnaire design and pilot the analysis with the questionnaire.

Identify the individuals to be questioned and obtain assurances of their co-operation from their managers if necessary.

The skills required for analysis of written questionnaires are different from those required for face-to-face interviewing. Whatever methods are chosen, identify suitable personnel (and equipment).

Clarify the nature of the final report and agree any presentations required (for example to customer management).

Prepare a plan to review the progress of the survey and monitor whether it is staying within budget and on time.

Stage three: gathering and analyzing the answers

The activities involved at this stage, and the time and resources required for them, vary depending upon the method of data collection chosen.

Written questionnaires Completed by individuals on their own, these are a good means to collect precise information from a large number of people at once. Their major disadvantage is that many people fail to return such questionnaires. A response rate of 50 per cent is average, and to achieve 85 per cent extremely good. To increase the response rate:

* secure agreement from managers that their staff will complete a questionnaire

* include a covering letter explaining the advantages of completing the questionnaire to the respondent, describing the uses to which the information will be put, and repeating the date by which the questionnaire should be returned and to whom it should be returned

* have the questionnaire prepared so that it is well presented, clearly laid out, and looks simple and quick to fill in

* monitor the responses, report on the response rate, prompt respondents just before the questionnaires are due to be returned, and again just after (for those who failed to return them).

Normally, allow only a few weeks for respondents to complete and return the questionnaires. A longer period is unlikely to increase the response rate. Exceptions to this are questionnaires which ask the respondents to record incidents over a specific period of time before completing the questionnaire; for example a request to record the number of times response from the computer terminal was poor over a specific two-week period, and to describe the effect on the person's work.

Prepare for the analysis of the results whilst waiting for the respondents to return the questionnaires. Ensure that the tools to aid analysis are available. The following are suitable:

* a spreadsheet with graphics on a personal computer

* a database with report writer and graphics (many Information Centres support these).

Sophisticated statistical analysis (standard deviations etc) requiring specialist tools is unlikely to be required for a customer satisfaction questionnaire. That level of detailed analysis is normally not necessary or cost effective.

Check the completed questionnaires for errors or omissions as soon as they are returned, and correct them if possible. Enter the replies into the spreadsheet in batches as they are ready. Analysis should not be time consuming once the data has been entered, but do allow time to return to the questionnaires and analyze them in other ways than those originally planned - answers may be unexpected and prompt further analysis.

Telephone interviews   As with a written questionnaire there is usually a set of specific questions to be asked, but with a limited range of possible answers. Design the questions carefully so that they are of a type that can be answered immediately, without much thought. The Help Desk is well placed to undertake this type of survey, and to analyze the results.

As with written questionnaires, obtain the agreement of the customer managers prior to carrying out the survey and send an explanatory letter to all prospective interviewees.

Analyze the results in the same way as for written questionnaires.

Face-to-face interviews

This type of interview is the most flexible way to collect information. Both the interviews and the analysis of results are, however, very time consuming.

The interviewer must be careful not to influence responses from the interviewees, and must be seen to be objective. Consider whether it is more appropriate to use staff other than IT personnel; for example training or personnel staff or external consultants, to carry out the interviews. However the impartiality this option provides, must be weighed against possible lack of subject knowledge among the interviewers.

Allow adequate time for:

* setting up appointments for interviews (key people have very full diaries)

* carrying out the interviews (approximately one hour each plus any travelling time)

* writing up the interview, from tape recordings or written notes (1-2 hours each)

* analyzing the results of all the interviews.

Group discussions

These have the advantage of taking little of the respondents' time, particularly if the request for information is just one item on the agenda of a regular meeting such as a user group. However, group discussions are very unpredictable, cannot give statistical results and are liable to be dominated by one or two voluble people. In addition, the attendees may not be representative of customers as a whole. Planning for group discussions is very simple, the stages being:

* convene the group or add the item to an agenda, inform participants of the questions/topics of discussion and ask them to give the matter some consideration in advance of the meeting

* attend the group meeting and guide the discussion to ensure that everyone has a say

* write up the results from notes or a tape recording.

Whichever method of gathering information is used, always inform respondents what is going to happen to their replies. Otherwise there is a danger of them assuming that everything they have stated will be acted upon immediately. Face-to-face interviewers and leaders of group discussions must make clear that they do not have the authority to promise immediate action, and that the normal procedures must still be followed with regard to changes and problems.

Stage four: interpreting and reporting

Whatever the type of survey, present the results in a written report. If face-to-face interviews or group discussions have been used, the report is likely to be full of qualitative detail and specific examples of respondents' opinions and perspectives. Questionnaires, whether written or telephoned, produce results that are more quantitative, (though some anecdotes can be collected from open-ended questions). Consider presenting the results graphically to make them immediately comprehensible. Guidelines for report structures are given in Annex D4.

Allow time for discussion, review and redrafting of the report; the report does not just present the findings, but also interprets them and describes their consequences. Involve the report writer(s), the commissioners of the survey, and the customer and IT managers who were consulted during stage one, in this process.

3.1.4.2 Customer care programmes

Sir Colin Marshall said that when he arrived at British Airways in 1983 he found a technically excellent airline where passengers had come to be regarded almost as an irritant. No doubt there are many other examples where service providers seem to regard customers as a nuisance. The attitude is also observed in some IT Services organizations, with customers' demands blamed for disrupting IT schedules.

Standards of service that may have been tolerated a number of years ago are no longer acceptable. Customers increasingly expect not only quality services but also quality support for these services. Customers expect the provider to make a systematic effort to understand their true needs, to be courteous, to listen to them and to solve any problems they have in using the service.

Customers are usually prepared to pay for a quality service but more and more are finding that poor services are not worth having at all - at any price. Quality IT service provision and support to customers are essential to meeting the business needs of IT customers and the IT service provider in a cost effective manner.

Changing the culture of IT Services from production to customer service, requires a substantial shift in attitudes, and an investment in education and development of IT Services staff. One way to undertake this change is to mount a customer care programme, known by a variety of names like 'Client First', 'Every Customer Counts', 'Customer Service'. Senior management commitment to the programme is essential to its success. Impetus to improve customer service must come from the top of the organization.

Do not confine the programme to front-line staff, those who come into direct contact with customers during their work. The courtesy and professionalism of front-line staff is important, but delivery of IT services to customers depends for its success on many people doing their part well, not only those with whom the customer has direct contact. Ensure that all IT Services staff are aware of how their actions help or hinder the goal of satisfying customers' requirements.

Consider IT Services participating in a wider customer care programme, including all IT staff, or all Management Services staff rather then initiating its own.

When planning a customer care programme there are four main stages:

* diagnosis and preparation

* management commitment and planning

* programme implementation

* review and reinforcement.

Stage one: diagnosis and preparation

Establish the broad purpose of the programme. Start by ascertaining the current quality of IT services and the customer perspective of, and satisfaction with, these services (see 3.1.2.3 and 3.1.4.1). Further investigation may also be necessary to establish the baseline cost of IT service failures and deficiencies; and to get actual examples of poor service.

Use written questionnaires plus a number of interviews with selected customers to get the required information and understanding.

Establishing the baseline cost

The baseline costs of IT service failures to the organization are described in more detail at Annex E1. They include:

* lost business opportunities and loss of revenue or profits

* business or contract penalties imposed on the IT service provider's customers within the organization, for failing to deliver to their customers

* time lost by customers as a result of service interrupts, failures and deficiencies

* time spent correcting errors and repeating poor work within IT Services

* time spent on both sides reporting and discussing problems and failures

* the cost of discarding materials and equipment which is no longer functioning to the required standard.

These costs cannot be determined with 100 per cent accuracy. However the effort of specifying the financial consequences of IT service failures and problems is salutary and educational and the costs can provide a reasonable indication of areas for improvement. IT service providers must be aware of their customers' priorities and the cost impact of failure.

If no staff time recording system is in place, all IT Services staff need to record the time they spend on these activities over say a two or three week period to gather this information.

Collect examples of poor service by IT Services. Especially useful are occurrences that might seem trivial to IT staff, but are highly inconvenient to customers. Common examples are poor handling of telephone calls and instances demonstrating the 'not my problem' attitude.

As an example of the kind of information to be sought, British Gas circulated a brief customer satisfaction questionnaire including the question 'What is it that most irritates you about the service British Gas provides'. Responses included vague appointments, taking too long to answer the phone, engineers being slow to complete work, and high prices. British Gas published these results, alongside more positive responses for maintaining gas supply and attending to gas leaks (amongst others), and mentioning the improvements they are making to remove these irritations.

Produce a report

Customer liaison staff need to discuss with senior IT managers and other parts of the IT Directorate the costs and timescales of implementing a customer care programme and then produce a report which:

* describes customer satisfaction and dissatisfaction with the IT services provided

* estimates the costs and risks emanating from poor customer service

* sets out initial broad objectives for a customer care programme intended to address the problems identified, and how it might be implemented

* considers the practicality of IT Services alone carrying out the programme, or the reasons for extending it to a wider group; for example all IT, or all Management Services

* provides first estimates of the benefits, costs and timescales of a programme.

Submit the report to senior IT management and, if they are content (see stage 2), publish appropriate highlights, particularly the findings on customer satisfaction and plans of what is being recommended.

Stage two: management commitment and planning

At this stage customer liaison staff give a presentation of the report to senior IT management. Detailed discussions are then needed to:

* consider the results of stage one, and accept the report in part or total

* define, redefine or re-iterate the mission statement for IT Services, a clear simple statement of the aims of IT Services

* identify gaps between the current IT services provided and the ideal, as defined by the mission statement

* specify improvements required, and outline the programme necessary to implement these improvements

* devise a title for the customer care programme, appropriate to the mission statement for the organization

* define the component parts of the programme and agree detailed objectives and terms of reference for each

* designate responsibility for carrying out the parts of the programme.

These discussions are intensive and demanding, since they involve self examination and some innovative thinking. Given the concentration required, try to arrange dedicated one or two day sessions away from the working environment, to avoid interruptions and to facilitate informal discussions which can continue through breaks and mealtimes.

Senior management commitment is of the utmost importance to the success of a customer care programme. It is demonstrated by the time given to these initial discussions by senior management. Do not undertake the customer care programme until this commitment is forthcoming even if it means substantial delay.

As part of the programme, consider the need to review the IT organization's policies on:

* recruitment for IT Services staff, to place emphasis on a customer-caring attitude and good communications skills, as well as technical skills, at least in certain posts

* induction training for new staff, to include an understanding of the mission statement and the customer service perspective

* staff performance evaluation, to include personal and communication skills alongside technical skills

* team performance targets, to stress the importance of meeting customers' business needs, as embodied in service level agreements

* charging customers, and any rebates for poor service

* internal communications, to ensure that IT staff are briefed about customer perceptions, and their own performance (including major successes and failures) and that they work together with common aims

* quality management and the promotion of a quality culture

* commitment of senior management time to customer care.

Consider which policies need to be reflected in a customer care programme. If there are any conflicting interests between current policies and the programme, consider modifying the policies.

This stage is completed, and the programme is ready for launching, when senior IT management has:

* agreed the overall objectives of the programme

* identified all the component parts of the programme and set objectives for each (these components may include, for example, investigation and commitment to required action on any of the policies mentioned above, training sessions)

* identified responsibilities and timescales, and committed resources for each element of the programme

* agreed a plan for the programme as a whole, and obtained financial approval for its cost, for example training

* set up a Steering Group of senior IT managers to manage the programme.

Customer liaison staff are responsible throughout this stage for documenting all discussions, improvement ideas and decisions taken, and for drafting documents, for example the programme plan. Customer liaison staff convene the Steering Group and provide the secretary.

Stage three: programme implementation

IT Services staff become personally involved in the customer care programme at this stage.

Programme implementation, managed by the Steering Group, consists of:

* telling all IT Services staff about the mission statement, the current failures and the improvements sought (perhaps using a training session)

* setting up task forces or improvement action teams to investigate the policies and areas previously identified and specify changes to be made

* encouraging all staff to contribute suggestions for improving the services provided by IT; for example by quality circles (see Annex E4)

* ensuring that customers are made aware, via their management, of the IT Services customer care initiative and

  - are clear on what it is being implemented

  - are clear on the expected timetable for achieving improvements

  - are encouraged to provide constructive feedback on progress to customer liaison staff

* monitoring progress made and reporting to all staff

  - actions being taken by senior management; for example as a result of task force recommendations

  - outstanding examples of improved service and/or contributions from teams or individuals, and the value of these improvements

  - any evidence of improvements to customer satisfaction with IT services; for example fewer complaints

  - any new problems or failures which come to light

* relaying the message, via staff bulletins, newsletters, newspapers, posters and any other means available, that service to customers matters.

Annex E describes in more detail some of the techniques to use during the implementation of a customer care programme; for example task forces, quality circles.

Implementation of a customer care programme can involve a substantial investment of staff time including:

* senior management, to attend Steering Group meetings and to describe the mission and the programme objectives at training sessions

* task force members to carry out their investigations and deliberations

* all IT Services staff to attend training sessions and to work on improvements

* customer liaison staff to organize and run the programme on a day-to-day basis.

Consider whether outside training or consultancy expertise is required to run the training sessions, if the number of staff involved is large or the expertise is not available in-house.

Stage four: review and reinforcement

Review the programme after approximately one year, or at the time the training and task force activities are completed if that is earlier.

Reappraise the costs of IT service failures (as described in Annex E1), on the same basis as previously, in the expectation that there has been a reduction. However, new factors may have influenced the overall costs. These need to be taken into account and any necessary actions to reduce new costs identified.

Produce a report which includes:

* what has been achieved by the programme

* what problems were encountered

* what resources have been involved in the programme

* what ongoing work to improve customer service has been identified as a result of the programme

* proposals on how to monitor the continuing impact and results of the programme, and who is to be allocated the responsibility for carrying out the monitoring.

The Steering Group meets to receive the report and agree the ongoing activities and responsibilities. Communicate all improvements achieved to all IT Services staff and customers.

Although the customer care programme is now complete, the IT Services Manager retains overall responsibility for continuing customer care, and for continuing to improve customer service (for example as ongoing customer support activities).

3.1.4.3 Publicity for IT Services

An essential element of improving customer relations is giving IT Services a human face. One cannot expect to improve relationships with customers if all they see of IT Services appears on a screen, and if they do not know the individuals involved in providing and supporting the IT services. Equally one cannot expect customers to make the best use of IT services unless they know exactly what services are on offer, and what they have to do to gain access to them.

A publicity drive by customer liaison staff is required if it is apparent that customers are not aware of:

* the people they should contact in IT Services (for example if the Help Desk is being underused or bypassed)

* the full range of IT services available to them, and how to access these services (for example procedures for access to the mainframe)

* the successes of IT Services (failings are usually noticed)

* new services on offer

* plans for future improvements, and when they are expected to be implemented.

A publicity drive is likely to be a small initiative, too small to warrant the use of PRINCE, and well within the capability of one person alongside his or her other responsibilities. However, it is important to allocate responsibility for the drive and to make adequate time available if it is to succeed.

There are three stages to the planning and implementation of a publicity drive.

Stage one: define the message

Be clear what is to be said, and to whom. It is important to view the message from the perspective of the recipient.

When publicizing a new service:

* describe how it benefits the customer

* make clear how access to the service is gained, and how customers can find out more about it

* explain any restrictions upon its use, and any restraints customers must observe as users

* give details of demonstrations they can attend.

When publicizing improvements to services, similar strictures apply - see it from the customers' point of view and describe the difference it will make to them, not to you. Describe the benefits the customer will experience.

When publicizing existing services more widely, seek the co-operation of existing customers. If they are willing to talk to prospective customers, or demonstrate the services to them, this can be a great help. Remember IT Services may be the only point of contact between disparate groups of customers, who might not otherwise come into contact with each other.

Define who is to be contacted, and their location.

Stage two: choose the medium and prepare the message

Choose an appropriate medium for publicizing the message. Consider the following:

* organization-wide bulletins, newsletters, office notices or staff newspapers

* items on the agenda of user groups

* arranged demonstrations, at which attendance is voluntary

* electronic messages direct to all current users

* a display of posters in customer workplaces, or more public places such as staff restaurants

* the issue of credit-card-size guide cards; for example with the Help Desk number (these can be self-adhesive, to stick on terminals for reference).

Choose the most graphic medium possible - if a service is being promoted, try to give the audience direct experience of it. If people are to be introduced try to arrange for the audience to meet them even if the intention is that customers should subsequently phone or write to them.

The choice is also influenced by the time and budget available. It is important that all printed materials (posters, bulletins) are well presented, but professional preparation can be expensive unless in-house printing facilities are available. Use existing facilities, where possible, to keep the cost down.

The preparation time depends upon the medium chosen and the intended size of the audience. Prepare the message in good time, and check it carefully before issue.

Stage three: issue the publicity

Broadcast the message, through the chosen medium. Monitor the results of the publicity drive by direct contact with a number of intended recipients. See if they got the message and ascertain their reaction. Repeat or modify as appropriate.

Finally, produce a brief report on the publicity drive for IT Services management, stating:

* the message conveyed

* the audience, intended and actual

* the media used

* the costs incurred

* the results.

Ensure that any deficiencies are traced back to source and rectified.

3.2 Dependencies

The major dependencies for planning and introducing customer liaison are:

* Help Desk, change management and service level management either in place within the IT Services organization or planned and introduced concurrently with customer liaison

* senior IT management commitment which involves

  - IT Services allocating resources (staff and time) to help and support customers - the resources can be built up gradually as customer liaison achieves successes - and to improve liaison with the customers

  - IT Services management ensuring that all problems identified via customer liaison activities are put right at source

* customer management's willingness to co-operate with customer liaison staff and to allocate time for customer staff to spend on liaison activities such as attending liaison meetings and completing questionnaires

* the availability of accurate management information on IT services, for example service level statistics and costs, on a regular basis and acceptance of this information by customers and IT staff

* a co-operative relationship between customer liaison staff and application development and maintenance teams, in particular with

 - application development staff working on development projects where customer liaison co-ordinates much of IT Services' involvement

 - application maintenance staff, who must accept that increased liaison with customers can lead to an increase in the number of changes requested in the short-term

 - both development and maintenance staff, who must recognize the importance of producing and maintaining documentation to match the systems

* the attitude of IT staff and management - good customer service requires positive thinking, concentrating on improvements, not apportioning blame

* the importance of customer service being taken into account in staff recruitment and training

* support systems within IT Services to allow fast production of memos and other documentation on customer contacts.

Where customers are widely distributed geographically, customer liaison is logistically more difficult and absorbs more resources.

3.3   People

Customer liaison affects not only IT Services staff but other staff within the IT Directorate such as applications development personnel. Senior IT management must promote the philosophy to all their staff that 'customer service counts'.

3.3.1 The IT Services Manager

The IT Services Manager has overall responsibility for customer liaison and must back the customer service philosophy and maintain contacts with the key senior customer managers.

The IT Services Manager must ensure that all IT staff who may come into contact with customers are educated in the principles of professional contact and that customer liaison personnel are properly trained.

3.3.2 Delegation of responsibilities

Depending on the size of the organization, the IT Services Manager should plan to delegate the following aspects of customer liaison to one or more managers within the IT Services section:

* customer support, either nominating one person (for example the Service Level Manager) as Customer Liaison Manager for all customers, or nominating a different manager as Customer Liaison Manager for each distinct group of customers (for example branch customers, head office customers etc)

* project management of initiatives to improve customer relations

* liaising with existing or new customers on the implementation of a new service or with a new group of customers on their take-on to use an existing service.

3.3.3 Organizational structures

Two possible organizational structures, suitable for different size IT organizations, are given at figures 2 and 3 opposite.

Figure 2 shows how to organize a very large IT Services section (say with approximately 5,000 customers and 250 IT Services staff). For such a very large section consider the need for a separate Customer Liaison Manager, particularly if customers are situated at a number of locations.

In a large organization (say with approximately 3000 customers and 150 IT Services staff) consider combining the roles of Customer Liaison Manager and Service Level Manager in one post.

In a smaller IT Services section (with approximately 50 IT services staff), responsibility for customer liaison might be allocated to several managers. Figure 3 illustrates how customer liaison responsibilities can be split in an organization with local offices and a headquarters.

**Figure 2:
Responsibility for
customer liaison in a
very large IT Services
Section**

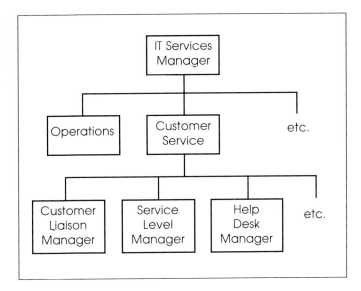

**Figure 3:
Responsibility for
customer liaison in a
smaller IT Services
Section**

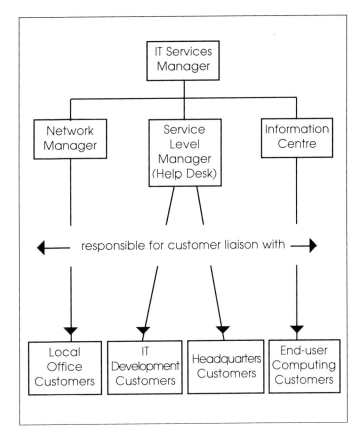

3.3.4 Customer liaison staff

Customer liaison is an important element in effective service provision and business support. Bear in mind when giving staff specific responsibilities for customer liaison, that they need to have, or acquire, an overview of the IT services provided and an understanding of how IT is used in the business. Consider giving staff with little understanding of the customer area, a brief secondment to familiarize themselves. Alternatively, second or recruit staff from the customer side.

Customer liaison staff need communication, organizational and problem solving skills. Good interviewing technique and the ability to contribute effectively to meetings are also desirable. They must be capable of taking a proactive role, and ensuring that improvements identified as a result of customer liaison activities are carried out. Some technical knowledge is desirable, but more important is the ability to communicate about technical issues in customers' language without using computer jargon.

Important qualities for customer liaison staff are persistence, confidence, patience and commitment to what they are doing. They should also be sympathetic to customer problems, a good listener, and perceptive. A pleasing personality is also a useful asset.

3.3.5 Training

Customer liaison staff must be trained in the techniques and procedures covered in section 3.1. All IT Services staff who may come into contact with customers must be trained in the principles of professional contact with customers. Training, as an integral part of a customer care programme, for all IT Services staff, is described at Annex E2. The IT Services Manager should review other training, especially the induction training of new IT staff, to ensure that the customer service message is clear and that IT staff develop a positive attitude towards customers.

3.3.6 Customer contacts

The customers involved in liaison with IT Services, and the nature of the contacts, are described in Annex B.

3.4   Timing

Guidance is given at 3.1.2.2, 3.1.2.3 and 3.1.2.4 on how and when to introduce customer liaison (in terms of implementing customer support, professionalism of contacts and customer liaison initiatives) in the following types of situation:

*   a greenfield installation or one where formal IT infrastructure management functions are not in operation

*   an installation where the basic IT infrastructure management functions are in operation

*   where new systems or services are being introduced or new customers are being taken on.

The procedures to ensure professional handling of all IT Services contacts with their customers may be introduced at any time.

Building close and co-operative relationships with customers is not a fast process - expect it to take a good deal of time, up to two years, especially if starting from a base of poor relations in the past.

Do not undertake a major initiative on customer liaison when it is already known that there are significant deficiencies in the level of service being provided to customers. Direct effort to correcting these first.

Aim to complete most customer liaison initiatives within as short a time as possible, in order to maintain momentum. A customer satisfaction survey by written questionnaire should take no more than 2-3 months to complete, and by a simple telephone questionnaire only a few weeks.

A publicity drive should take less than one month to organize, although the publicity may be issued over a longer period. A customer care programme can take from several months to about a year depending on the objectives and the size of the organization.

4. Implementation

4.1 Procedures

The following sub-sections describe the bringing into service of customer liaison activities within an IT Services section.

4.1.1 Ongoing customer liaison

At the outset, inform all IT Services and customer staff about the new procedures. Tell these staff how the new procedures will affect them. Train everyone concerned, in the new procedures as planned.

4.1.1.1 Customer support

Implement customer support on a phased basis. Pilot it with a customer community with which relations appear to have been reasonably good in the past, but move within a few months onto those customers with whom poor relations are felt to exist.

Manage customer expectations carefully. Make cost and resource constraints clear. Do not lead customers to expect improvements to be made as soon as they have been identified and understood by IT Services. However, do let users know what is happening about their difficulties and when corrective action can be expected.

The critical issue at implementation is that everyone affected understands the purpose of customer support. Spend adequate time with key individuals, on both the customer and the IT Services side, to gain their co-operation. Some may feel threatened by the introduction of a customer support role, and skilful handling is required.

Customer liaison staff need to be made aware of all non-routine contacts between customers and IT Services staff, for example complaints, unusual queries. Instruct all IT Services staff that a copy of any documentation regarding such contacts (for example call reports, minutes, letters) must be sent to customer liaison staff. The documentation must make clear whether the customer enquiry is being dealt with or is for actioning by customer liaison staff. Instruct Help Desk and customer liaison staff to process complaints via the problem management system. Make customer liaison staff responsible for following up the complaints and getting them resolved.

Keep customer liaison staff informed of the outcome of regular meetings on service levels and changes, by including them on the distribution list of minutes of such meetings.

Customer liaison staff should thus receive continuous information about the service received by customers and their responses to it. They must act quickly, on information received, to show that sending it is useful. Otherwise the stream of information will dry up.

Start regular liaison meetings. Expect the first of them to take rather longer than those held later, until the agenda settles down into a regular pattern and until customer liaison staff become familiar with the customers' businesses and uses of IT, and customers get to know IT Services' procedures. An informal setting may be helpful for the initial meetings, while people get to know each other.

Management of customer complaints (other than black and white incidents, which are the Help Desk's responsibility) begins with encouraging the customers to inform the Help Desk of any inadequacies in the provision of IT services, and to make constructive suggestions for improvements. The Help Desk must pass on complaints and suggestions to customer liaison staff, through the problem management system and the Problem Manager. Management of customer expectations is very important here. Explain to customers that they may be asked to substantiate complaints and that some improvements, whilst desirable, cannot be implemented quickly or at all, because of cost or resource constraints. Give particular encouragement to low-cost/ high-yield improvement suggestions. Customer liaison staff need to act upon these suggestions constructively and quickly to encourage more suggestions.

Achieving results early is the key to the successful implementation of customer support. Solving a vague or long-standing problem rapidly, or progressing the early stages of a request for change quickly, will demonstrate the value of customer liaison.

4.1.1.2 Professional customer contacts

Ensure that all tools and facilities needed to implement the new procedures for professionally handling contacts with customers are available. Complete any procurement required, and carry out related training. Test the facilities before the procedures become mandatory.

Issue the new procedures to all IT management and staff who are required to use them well before the date they become mandatory. If there is to be a pilot involving only part of IT Services, issue the procedures to the people involved and extend coverage to other staff when the pilot has been successfully completed. Piloting should be necessary only if the procedures require major changes in current practice, or involve the introduction of significant new tools or facilities. Finalize staff's training in the new procedures, before they are required to use the procedures.

Issue the procedures to key customer managers who liaise with IT Services, inform them that they can insist on the standards being followed, and encourage them to report any breaches of procedure to nominated customer liaison staff.

Encourage both IT Services and customer staff to make constructive suggestions for improvement in the procedures. Deal with these through the change management system. Make clear to everyone that the procedures will be regularly reviewed, and can be improved if IT staff and customers provide feedback.

There may be a perception that an additional bureaucratic burden is being imposed upon IT Services staff, and it is therefore important to explain to them why the new procedures are being introduced if they are to be successfully adopted.

4.1.2 Customer liaison initiatives

Plans for implementing customer liaison initiatives, specifying implementation dates and timescales, must be drawn up and agreed well in advance of implementation. Where several initiatives are being undertaken, make clear their relative priority. Put the plans into action as specified. Monitor and report progress as laid down in PRINCE, for initiatives that are carried out as PRINCE projects.

Details of the implementation stages of customer liaison initiatives can be found as follows:

*   customer satisfaction questionnaires in stages three and four of 3.1.4.1

*   customer care programmes in stages three and four of 3.1.4.2

*   publicity drives in stage two of 3.1.4.3.

4.2   Dependencies

Implementing customer liaison as an ongoing function and undertaking specific initiatives are not technically complex processes. They are not dependent on the authorization of large expenditure on hardware or new computer systems. The crucial dependencies are all to do with people, and these are:

* commitment from senior IT management, shown by their willingness to

    - liaise with senior customer management

    - progress initiatives to improve customer relations

    - emphasize customer service at all opportunities

    - follow customer liaison procedures

    - ensure customer queries and difficulties are followed up and that all appropriate action is taken to tackle problems at source

* co-operation from customer and IT middle management and staff

* identification of suitable staff to work on customer liaison

* positive attitudes from IT and customer staff, concentrating on improvements, not blame for failures.

Ensure that the support systems and tools that were identified at the planning stage are available and have been tested before implementation takes place.

4.3   People

People are the key to the successful implementation of customer liaison. Ensure that management responsibility for customer liaison has been allocated, and that customer liaison staff have been assigned their roles.

Ensure that customer liaison staff have been properly trained. Have all IT Services staff trained in the procedures required for professional contacts with customers. Implement training for other IT Services staff, that is planned as part of a customer care programme, at the implementation stage of the programme.

4.4 Timing

Start to implement ongoing customer liaison activities as soon as possible after management commitment has been gained. Avoid busy periods for IT or customer staff, holiday periods, and times when major reorganizations or personnel changes are planned.

5. Post-implementation and audit

5.1 Procedures

For the ongoing operation of customer liaison activities, use the procedures planned as described in section 3.1. The following sub-sections describe the ongoing management and control of these customer liaison activities. There is guidance on:

* monitoring and reviewing the effectiveness of on going customer liaison

* reviewing customer liaison initiatives

* auditing customer liaison procedures and activities

* planning for the future.

5.1.1 Monitoring customer liaison

The Customer Liaison Manager or the IT Services Managers who have been allocated responsibilities for customer liaison should:

* continuously monitor the ongoing activities of customer support, the procedures implemented for customer contacts and any customer liaison initiatives which are in progress

* investigate any problems affecting customer liaison activities which are discovered

* initiate actions necessary to prevent the recurrence of these problems.

Remember that these tasks may involve the need to liaise with other IT Services managers as well as with customers.

Report progress with customer liaison activities regularly (normally monthly), to both the IT Services Manager and customer managers. Highlight current and forecast problems, and plans for tackling them, as well as achievements. In each month's report indicate progress in dealing with problems identified in the previous month's report.

Review progress in dealing with customers at the quarterly meetings discussed in section 3.1.3.1. Take the opportunity to resolve difficulties and differences and to look forward to future opportunities and problems. Agree required actions and check at the next meeting that these have been carried out.

5.1.2 Reviewing ongoing customer liaison

The IT Services Manager should review customer liaison activities and procedures on a regular basis to:

* measure their effectiveness

* identify inadequacies in the procedures

* examine problems which have been encountered

* consider what improvements have been achieved since the previous review

* consider any trends which are identified

* identify changes needed to deal with current and forecast difficulties and changes in usage.

Document the results of these reviews in a report to the Director of IT and service customer managers.

5.1.2.1 Customer support

Carry out a review of the support being provided to each group of customers once the customer liaison function has been in operation for them for approximately six months, and at least annually thereafter. Cover in the review:

* the level of usage by customers of the customer support service, and the trend in usage

* senior IT and customer management commitment

* are customers' needs being properly supported?

* the IT staff's attitude to customers - has it become more positive?

* have IT staff gained a better understanding of the part IT Services play in meeting the business needs of the organization and of future customer plans?

* training of IT staff in customer support activities

* the level of co-operation from IT management and staff outside IT Services, to the customer support activities

* availability of customer training in the use of IT services

* the level of understanding by customers of current and future IT Services' plans

* the general co-operation of customers and their active participation

* customer care programmes initiated

* communications within IT and with customers.

An essential part of reviewing the effectiveness of customer support is measuring the specific aspects which were identified at the planning stage as useful indicators of effectiveness. Specific measures can include:

* the number of complaints from customers received by the Help Desk

* the number of requests for advice to the Help Desk

* the time taken to process customer problems passed on by the Help Desk to customer liaison staff

* the number of customer problems identified as originating in the customer area, for example as a result of inadequate training in the use of equipment

* the number of customer comments on changes to services proposed by IT Services

* the number of customer-initiated changes

* the level of customer satisfaction with IT services.

Produce a report for senior IT and customer management. In addition to documenting the results of the review and specific measures of effectiveness, cover in the report:

* the IT service(s) provided to each group of customers

* the customer liaison activities carried out, the improvements implemented as a result, the benefits gained and how many customers were involved

* any problems with customer liaison procedures or deliverables reported, and requests for change submitted as a result

* the objectives for customer liaison for the following year, taking into account new work, new customers, customers' plans and past deficiencies

* the customers' priorities for IT service improvements

* progress since the last review.

The IT Services Manager produces the report in consultation with customer managers or the Customer Co-ordinator. Customers are thus involved in defining the service improvements to which they give top priority, and in reviewing the effectiveness of the customer liaison function.

5.1.2.2 Professional customer contacts

Undertake a review of procedures for contacts with customers of IT Services after the procedures have been in operation for a few months and then at least annually thereafter. Include as part of the review selective interviews with IT staff and customers, checks on documentation and minutes and examination of records.

Invite all staff who are required to follow the procedures to contribute, to the review, suggestions for constructive improvements. The IT Services Manager produces a brief report for customer and IT management on the findings of the review, describing changes to the procedures recommended as a result. Allow for minor procedural changes between major reviews, but these must be subject to change management control.

IT Services managers must follow the procedures themselves and not feel that they are exempt because of their seniority. It is important that they set a good example of how to treat customers.

5.1.3 Reviewing customer liaison initiatives

Customer liaison projects using the PRINCE methodology are subject to post-implementation review as part of the project. Other initiatives need to be reviewed on a similar basis.

When an initiative has been completed the IT Services Manager allocates the task of carrying out a review to a suitable manager. The review needs to cover:

* the effectiveness of the initiative

    - to what extent did it achieve its desired objective?

    - what problems were encountered and how where they overcome

    - what improvements can be introduced if the initiative is repeated

* how efficiently was the initiative planned, conducted and managed, and what lessons if any can be learned for future initiatives.

Depending on the type of the initiative a further review or reviews may be needed to check whether improvements achieved have been sustained and verify that problems which were resolved have not recurred. If possible carry out such reviews as part of the annual review of ongoing customer liaison (5.1.2).

5.1.3.1 Customer satisfaction surveys

After a customer satisfaction survey, the IT Services Manager needs to review its effectiveness, and how efficiently it was conducted.

Judge the effectiveness of a survey against its original objectives. Answer the following questions:

* did the survey fulfil its purpose and achieve its objectives?

* has it provided correct and comprehensive information about the quality of service?

* was a meaningful analysis of the results possible?

* how valuable does management perceive the results to be?

Judge how efficiently a customer satisfaction survey has been carried out, and the adequacy of the report of the findings, by considering the questions in the following checklist:

* were the objectives of the survey clear, and were they appropriate, given the uses to which the findings have been put?

* did the method selected to collect the information prove appropriate for what was required?

* who was asked for information and were they the appropriate people to provide it?

* of the people asked for information, how many responded and if the response was low (less than 75 per cent), do you consider that this might have introduced any bias into the findings?

* if the response was low, why was it low and how can it be improved next time?

* were the questions asked found to be unambiguous and well formed and were they appropriate to the survey objectives?

* did the timing of the survey appear to have any impact upon the results?

* were the answers clearly recorded and analysed and how many errors in responses were there?

* have the results been clearly documented - in tables and graphs if appropriate - and would further analysis of the answers give more information?

* are the conclusions of the report valid?

Do not repeat surveys too often in the same format, with the same respondents - repetition leads to a fall off in the response rate. If a survey needs to be repeated at a later date to evaluate the impact of changes made, use samples of the customer population to ensure that respondents are not asked to answer the same questions twice.

Instigate changes to deal with any deficiencies identified in the survey or the way in which it was carried out - where it is necessary for the effective completion of the present survey or appropriate to the conduct of future surveys.

5.1.3.2 Customer care programmes

There are four stages to a customer care programme which are described at 3.1.4.2. Stage four is 'Review and reinforcement' and guidance on reviewing a programme is given there.

Judge the success of a programme by the effects it has on the staff involved and their attitudes to their work and customers. Learn lessons from this programme for any future extensions to it and for any future programmes.

5.1.3.3 Publicity drives

Some time after a publicity drive review its effectiveness against its stated objectives. The timing of the review depends on the purpose of the drive; for example the publicity may be intended to result in immediate action on the part of the recipient or it may be giving advance notice of a new service.

In the review, answer the following general questions:

* did the audience find the publicity message useful?

* could the desired objective have been achieved more cost-effectively?

* did the publicity have the intended effect and produce the expected results?

When reviewing the efficiency of a publicity drive consider:

* has feedback indicated that the message was clear from a customer perspective and what proportion did it reach of the intended audience?

* was the audience selected the right one, with no omissions?

* was the expenditure kept as low as possible?

* was the publicity drive monitored as it happened and corrections made if they proved to be required?

* was the publicity drive properly documented and authorized?

Report on the review and instigate changes, emanating from it, to improve the conduct of future publicity drives.

5.1.4 Auditing customer liaison

Audit customer liaison activities for compliance with the agreed procedures and to examine the adequacy and effectiveness of the procedures in contributing to the quality of IT services. It is recommended that audits are carried out by independent audit staff and that they are done at least annually.

Consider the following general points in an audit:

* have terms of reference and objectives been drawn up for the customer liaison function?

* has responsibility for customer liaison been clearly allocated to one or more IT Services Managers?

* have the procedures been properly documented and agreed by IT and customer management as appropriate?

The auditors must produce a report for the IT Services Manager following the audit and discuss the results with the Customer Liaison Manager(s). All parties agree any remedial action necessary and when it is to be initiated and completed by.

For guidance on a general approach to auditing all infrastructure management activities please refer to the IT Infrastructure Library **Quality Audit** module. Guidance on auditing specific customer liaison activities is given below. Some of the information that has to be gathered for audits is the same as that required for reviews (5.1.2 - 5.1.3). Use such information for both purposes but take care to have it verified by the personnel conducting the reviews and audits.

5.1.4.1 Ongoing customer liaison

Audit customer support activities at least annually to check that laid-down procedures are being used. Check, in particular, that:

* adequate monitoring of activities has been carried out by customer liaison staff, and documented

* management information on IT services has been provided regularly to the appropriate Customer Liaison Manager(s) by other IT Services Managers

* regular and comprehensive reviews have been carried out, documented and reported to both IT and customer management

* recommendations and follow-up actions identified in reports and reviews have been actioned within an agreed timescale.

Examine the documentation relating to contacts with users to ensure that it is complete and follows the procedures laid down. The auditors also need to interview a number of IT Services' staff and customers to ensure that proper documentation is being maintained, and that verbal and telephone contacts are being conducted according to laid-down rules.

5.1.4.2 Customer liaison initiatives

Include completed customer liaison initiatives in an audit of ongoing customer liaison procedures. (If required, the advice given opposite can also be tailored for the auditing of liaison activities that are in progress).

Customer satisfaction survey

Carry out an audit by examining the survey report and through interviews with the manager for whom the survey was carried out, the person using the survey results, one or two respondents and, if applicable, someone who failed to return a response. Check that the documented procedures for customer satisfaction surveys have been followed, that the survey yielded the required information, and that follow-up actions have been or are being progressed as required.

Customer care programme

When auditing a customer care programme check the following:

* were the objectives of the programme set by senior IT management, clearly communicated to all participants?

* was the initial investigation of customer satisfaction and service failures thorough and honest?

* was implementation of the programme properly monitored and controlled by the Steering Group?

* were the recommendations resulting from stages one and two of the programme accepted and acted upon?

* did all staff participate in customer care programme sessions and were they all aware of the mission statement and the improvements to customer service aimed for?

* are all staff aware of the results of the programme?

* did IT Services management monitor the programme for effectiveness and take action to deal with any deficiencies?

Use independent personnel to audit customer care programmes. The programmes must leave a documented audit trail covering objectives, decisions, training sessions, implemented activities and monitoring and reviewing of the programmes post-implementation.

5.1.5 Forward planning

Once a customer liaison function is operating, it is essential that it is able to plan its future objectives and identify the staff resources needed to continue to fulfil its function effectively. It is important therefore that the Customer

Liaison Manager(s) is involved in forward planning in relation to IT systems and services, changes in customer requirements and changes in staffing levels.

Be prepared to instigate customer liaison initiatives from time to time to address the results of customer surveys, changes in the organization, senior management appointments, or IT Services reviews.

5.2 Dependencies

The major dependency for effective customer liaison is people and their level of commitment to customer liaison as a means to improve customer service. Reasonable stability of staff is also desirable - long-term relationships cannot be built with ever-changing people.

Another major long-term dependency is the availability of accurate management information, which is accepted by both customer and IT management, on the IT services which are provided.

Service Level Agreements, a Help Desk, and change management continue to be important in providing effective customer liaison.

5.3 People

The people involved in contacts between customers and IT Services, and the nature of these contacts, are described at Annex B.

The IT Services Manager has overall responsibility for customer liaison. The Customer Liaison Manager and/or other IT Services Managers who have been given responsibility for customer liaison, must regularly monitor activities for which they are responsible and review the effectiveness and efficiency of their activities or initiatives.

Involve customer managers in the reviews and provide senior customer management with copies of review reports.

Carry out audits using quality audit staff from the organization or an independent body.

5.4 Timing

Customer liaison is an ongoing process. Reviews may lead to new initiatives to improve customer relations, and responsibilities must be reorganized as appropriate.

The Customer Liaison Manager reviews progress of ongoing customer liaison with customers at the quarterly meetings discussed in section 3.1.3.1.

The IT Services Manager carries out a review of the support being provided to each group of customers once the customer liaison function has been in operation for them for approximately six months, and at least annually thereafter.

The IT Services Manager undertakes a review of procedures for contacts with customers of IT Services after they have been in operation for a few months and then at least annually thereafter.

The IT Services Manager allocates someone to review specific liaison initiatives once they have been completed and depending on the type of initiative a further review or reviews may be needed (see 5.1.3 for more guidance).

Staff independent of customer liaison should carry out audits of customer liaison activities at least annually.

6. Benefits, costs and possible problems

This section sets out the benefits of a customer liaison function, its costs and some possible problems.

6.1 Benefits

Liaison between IT service providers and customers is not optional, the option is how effectively to manage it. In today's competitive environment for IT service provision, IT Services Managers must take fully into account customers' requirements and must not ignore customer satisfaction.

Whilst some of the benefits of an effective customer liaison function can be intangible, implementing the guidance in this module will help bring about:

* the development of a co-operative partnership with customers

* an improved, professional approach to customer relationship by IT Services

* improved IT Services' understanding of customer perspectives.

Longer-term benefits which can be achieved are:

* an improved return on IT investment in the organization through the more effective use of IT by customers

* lower IT costs in the long-term in dealing with queries and complaints from customers

* higher customer satisfaction with IT Services and a better image for IT within the organization

* higher IT staff morale from clearer understanding of the uses to which IT is put, and from better relations with customers

* better educated customers, more able to exploit IT facilities.

For organizations using or considering using FM arrangements, this module provides useful guidance on the customer care that can be expected of the FM provider. Government departments that are CCTA customers should consult their procurement officer for guidance; a procurement and contracting service is available.

6.2   Costs

The costs involved in providing a customer liaison function are largely staff time and training costs. Little in the way of additional systems, tools or infrastructure should be required if Help Desk, service level management and change management are in place.

There will be extra initial costs to:

* investigate current customer satisfaction

* set up professional standards of contact

* plan and implement ongoing customer support

* instigate customer care initiatives.

However, these will reap benefits in the long-term.

Appointing a permanent Customer Liaison Manager is clearly expensive, given the mix of skills required, but can be justified in very large installations supporting a large number of customers. The approach of giving customer liaison responsibilities to existing IT Services Managers, is cost-effective in all organizations.

There may be a need for additional staff if customers are to be helped more extensively than before. It may be possible , however, to reallocate existing staff for such customer liaison duties. Experience shows that it is invariably more cost effective to provide help at an early stage than to address problems and difficulties later on.

Make particular initiatives, for example a customer care programme, the subject of individual investment appraisals.

6.3   Possible problems

Possible problems include:

* an inadequately defined role for customer liaison staff

* attempts to by-pass customer liaison staff

* raising of customers' expectations too high.

Clear terms of reference and agreement with both IT and customer senior managers before any customer liaison function is established, are crucial to overcoming these problems.

7. Tools

Few tools are needed to implement customer liaison; it is largely a matter of staff development and management. However tools to analyze customer survey responses (for example customized spreadsheets, graphics packages) are normally needed in an organization of any size. Word-processing facilities are required for efficient and timely production of documentation.

Customer liaison staff benefit if a Help Desk tool, and tools for change management and problem management, are in use within IT Services, in that accurate management information on incidents, problems, errors and changes affecting customers is available from these tools.

8. Bibliography

Information Systems Guide B1, The Users' Role in Systems
Development. CCTA.
Published by John Wiley & Sons, Chichester 1989.
ISBN 0 471 92526 8.

Information Systems Guide C1, Services Management.
CCTA.
Published by John Wiley & Sons, Chichester 1989.
ISBN 0 471 92534 9.

Information Systems Guide E4, Facilities Management.
CCTA.
Published by John Wiley & Sons, Chichester 1989.
ISBN 0 471 92547 0.

Annex A.   Glossary of terms

Acronyms and abbreviations used in this module

CRAMM	CCTA Risk Analysis and Management Method
FM	Facilities Management
IS	Information Systems
IT	Information Technology
PRINCE	Projects In Controlled Environments
SCT	Service Control Team
SLA	Service Level Agreement
SSADM	Structured Systems Analysis and Design Method

Definitions used in this module

Customer co-ordinator

A customer manager designated as IT Services' first line of contact with the customer base.

Facilities Management (FM)

The provision of the management, operation and support of an organization's computers and/or networks by an external source at agreed service levels. The service will generally be provided for a set time at agreed cost.

Greenfield installation

An IT facility, planned or newly installed, which does not replace an existing facility in the organization or location concerned.

Help Desk

The Help Desk is the single point of contact between IT Services and users (customers), or their representatives, on a day-to-day basis.

IT Services Manager

The person with overall responsibility for IT service quality. Typically his/her peers are the Applications Development Managers and the Administration and Finance Manager, and all are responsible to the organization's Director of IT.

PRINCE

The method adopted within government for planning, managing and controlling IS projects. It provides guidance on the management components (organization, plans and controls) and on the technical components (end products and the activities needed to produce them).

Service Control Team
(SCT)

A team of people, with skills roughly equivalent to business analysts, who will be responsible for managing an FM provider on behalf of the user organization.

Service Level Agreement
(SLA)

A written agreement or 'contract' between the users and the IT service provider which documents the agreed service levels for an IT service. Typically it will cover: service hours, service availability, customer support levels, throughputs and terminal response times, restrictions, functionality, and the service levels to be provided in a contingency. It may also include security and accounting policy.

Annex B. Contacts between customers and IT Services

In an IT Services section which has implemented formal IT infrastructure management, the majority of contacts between customers and the IT service providers will be handled by:

* the Help Desk, which has the main day-to-day contact, dealing with incidents and requests for help, and disseminating information

* the Service Level Manager, who manages the overall quality of IT service according to a contract (which is regularly reviewed and updated) agreed with the customers

* the director of IT and the IT Services Manager, who are involved in setting IT policies and IT strategy.

An overview of these contacts between customers and IT Services is shown at figure B1 below. Further detail on day-to-day contacts and on contacts including agreements and plans is given in figures B2 and B3, overleaf.

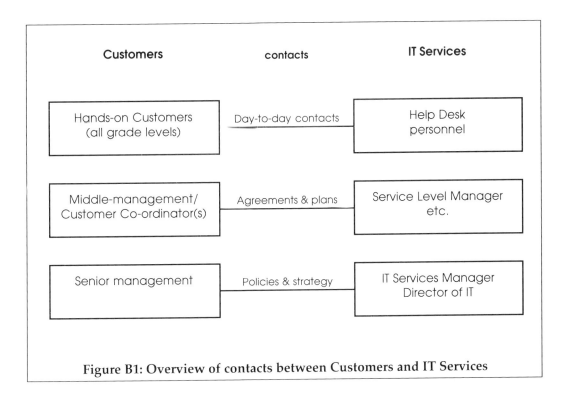

Figure B1: Overview of contacts between Customers and IT Services

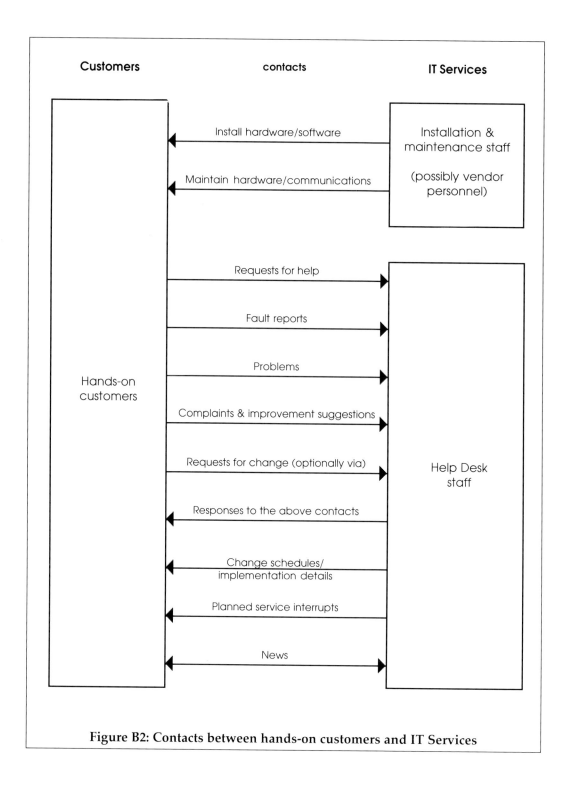

Figure B2: Contacts between hands-on customers and IT Services

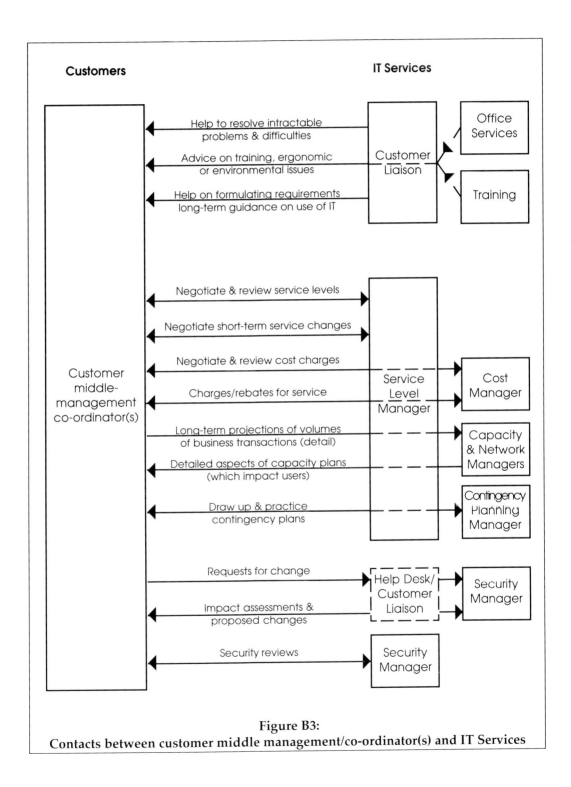

Figure B3:
Contacts between customer middle management/co-ordinator(s) and IT Services

B1 Categories of customers and type of contacts

The three broad categories of customers referred to in figure B1 above, and the type of contacts they have with IT Services are described in more detail at B2, B3 and B4.

Individual customers can be in more than one category; for example a senior manager can be a hands-on customer with a computer terminal on his or her desk and can also have responsibility for discussing with IT Services the implications of future business strategy.

Customer liaison personnel do not replace the IT Services contacts. They do however, have a role in monitoring the contacts, advising on best practices and ensuring that communication is as effective as possible. In some organizations the Service Level Manager and/or other IT Services Managers may also take on the role of Customer Liaison Manager(s) or be given part responsibility for customer liaison.

B2 Hands-on customers

For customers who are hands-on users of computer terminals, and/or recipients of print outs, the Help Desk is the major point of contact with IT Services. The Help Desk should be capable of dealing with calls from all grades or levels of staff about day-to-day issues that arise in using IT services. Installation and maintenance staff also have contact with hands-on customers, when installing or repairing terminals, though their visits may be scheduled through the Help Desk.

Examples of the types of contacts between hands-on customers and IT Services are shown in figure B2.

B2.1 Relationship between Help Desk and customer liaison

Customer liaison staff are concerned with the overall quality of all IT Services' contacts with customers, and may take initiatives to improve relations with customers. Help Desk staff should be included in any such initiatives (for example a customer care programme).

Customer liaison staff are also concerned with longer term, tactical relationships with customers, and with assisting them to make the best possible use of IT services available to them. The Help Desk can contribute to this by:

* providing customer liaison staff with information on IT service quality and service interrupts, from the user perspective

* logging and passing to customer liaison staff complaints and calls which require more extensive liaison with customers to resolve, and those which the Help Desk is not able to resolve to the customer's satisfaction

* providing a means of communicating direct to hands-on users to assist customer liaison staff to

  - publicize IT services

  - inform customers of customer liaison initiatives

  - gather customers' views, for example responses to questionnaires (verbal or written).

B3 Middle management or Customer Co-ordinator

Most management contact between IT service providers and customers takes place at middle management level, where detailed negotiations on service levels, changes and capacity plans take place. Good relations at this level are crucial to the long-term success of an IT service.

The User Assurance Co-ordinator role in a PRINCE project for the development of new systems is outlined at section 3.1.3.2. If this person is given a continuing co-ordinating role (Customer Co-ordinator) by the customer organization, after the system goes into live operation, then this person is ideal as a first point of contact for IT Services on service levels, problems, changes and any other matters concerning that particular system. A Customer Co-ordinator or someone fulfilling a similar role can also be valuable in resolving conflicts between different customers of the same system.

Examples of the types of contacts between customer middle management and/or a Customer Co-ordinator and IT Services, are shown at figure B3.

B3.1 Relationship between the Service Level Manager and customer liaison

Liaison with customers is often part of the Service Level Manager's responsibilities. Where this is not the case, customer liaison and service level management roles will be complementary. Customer liaison:

* sets standards for all contacts between customers and IT Services, which apply to service level reviews and other meetings

* provides expert assistance to customers to help them to specify their service level requirements, for existing and proposed services

* assists customers to resolve problems with service levels where the cause appears to be in the user domain, for example due to inadequate training

* assists in the resolution of incidents which impact service level targets, but which could not have been legislated for within the SLA

whilst service level management:

* provides detailed, concise and objective reports regularly to customers and customer liaison to show the achievements for each particular service

* regularly reviews service level achievements (say monthly) and SLAs (say every six months) with the senior customer managers who represent all the customers covered.

B3.2 Involvement of customer liaison personnel with change management

Customer liaison staff are concerned to ensure that customers make the best possible use of IT services and facilities, and may therefore:

* encourage customers to identify improvements to IT services and help them articulate their requirements as changes

* assist customers to evaluate and consider the impact of changes proposed by IT Services, or other customers

* assist customers to progress major changes that are beyond the authority of the CAB, for example the setting up of an Information Centre, or a new system procurement.

These functions may alternatively be part of the Change Manager's responsibilities.

B4 Senior management

Contacts between senior customer and IT management are largely concerned with IT strategy and long-term planning. Overall control, and the final approval of Service Level Agreements, capacity plans etc, lie with senior management. Terms of reference for service level management, Help Desk, change management and customer liaison, are agreed at this senior management level. Some of the issues raised by customer liaison staff may need resolution at this level.

B5 Internal IT section customers

IT Services management provide services and support not only to their business customers but to other parts of the IT organization such as application development and maintenance teams. Contacts between IT Services and other areas within the IT organization tend to be less formal than contacts with outside customers but effective customer liaison is just as important.

The three main aspects of customer liaison:

* ongoing customer support

* professionalism in contacts

* initiatives to improve customer service.

apply equally to internal relationships within the IT organization and customer liaison staff must be aware of their responsibilities to internal IT customers.

IT Services has to be involved whenever new services or applications are planned, or application or usage changes are envisaged. IT Services must take these changes into account, in their capacity, service and operations planning, to ensure that they are able to assist application developers and maintainers to make the best use of IT facilities available.

The quality of an IT service depends, amongst other things, on the quality of components of the service, including the quality of applications software. It is important that there is effective liaison between applications development and IT Services on such issues as hardware options, operator interfaces, recovery mechanisms, support diagnostics, Help Desk scripts, capacity requirements and running costs.

The IT Infrastructure Library **Application Life-cycle Support** module covers the responsibility of IT Services management regarding application development projects and subsequently for applications that have gone live and are subject to maintenance and enhancement.

The Finance and Administration section of the IT organization will inevitably be a customer of IT Services. Take into account their requirements and circumstances when planning a customer liaison function.

Annex C.   Customer survey questionnaires

C1   Purpose

Questionnaires have four main purposes:

* to collect the relevant responses

* to ensure responses are comparable

* to minimize bias

* to encourage the recipient to respond.

C2   Design

It is important when designing a questionnaire to consider what analysis is to be carried out on the results, and to ensure that all information collected is relevant to, and adequate to meet the objectives of the survey.

To encourage responses, ensure that a questionnaire is laid out clearly. Vary the format and type of question and include explanations to bridge changes of topic and explain their relevance. This is particularly important for any personal information required to put the respondents' answers in context.

C3   Questions

C3.1   Construction

Always construct questions very carefully. Ensure that the words used are unambiguous, and have the same meaning for all respondents. Frame questions in everyday language, or the respondents' business language, not technical computer language.

Include only questions which are essential to the objectives of the survey - resist the temptation to add other questions out of interest as they will confuse the respondent and reduce the response rate.

C3.2   Sequence

Consider the order of questions carefully. Make the early questions of interest to the respondent, and easy to answer, to encourage the respondent to continue. Put any questions that might be considered uninteresting towards the end. If any 'filter questions' are used, give very clear directions; eg "If 'yes' go on to question X".

C3.3   Types of question

Four main types of question can be included:

* dichotomous questions (with a 'yes' or 'no' answer)

* multiple choice questions

* open-ended questions

* rating scales.

Each type of question needs different preparation, and a different form of analysis.

Yes/No questions are easy to ask and answer, but need careful preparation to ensure that they are specific enough to allow only a clear yes or no answer.

Multiple-choice questions are interesting to answer, easy to analyze, but very difficult to design - the designer must know not only what to ask, but also all the possible answers, and must divide these answers into a comprehensive series of mutually exclusive categories.

Open-ended questions are easy to ask, but require more effort from the respondent, and are time consuming to analyze. The results are qualitative rather than quantitative, but they can increase the depth of information collected, and often provide useful quotes and comments for the survey report. Strictly limit the number of this type of question in a survey.

Rating scales are useful for gathering attitudes and opinions. Two examples of scales against which statements are rated follow:

* Scale One

  1   means agree strongly

  2   means agree

  3   means neither agree nor disagree

  4   means disagree

  5   means disagree strongly

* Scale Two

  1   means you personally believe the statement applies very little or not at all

  2   means you personally believe the statement applies to a limited extent

3   means you personally believe the statement
applies to a fair extent

4   means you personally believe the statement
applies to a considerable extent

5   means you personally believe the statement
applies to a very great extent.

The results are not strictly comparable, since the statements
may be interpreted variably by different respondents. They
can however, be used to explore subtle differences of
opinion and emphasis.

C4   Check the draft

Check all questions once written, to ensure they are specific
- check the who, what, where, when and how have all been
specified. For instance, rather than asking "How often is
System X used" ask "How many times have you looked at
the screen entitled ... in your office during the past week".
Also check for ambiguity, leading questions, loaded words
and generalizations (eg on average). Consider whether what
you are asking is reasonable.

C5   Produce the questionnaire

Produce the finished questionnaire as professionally as
possible within the cost constraints imposed. A
questionnaire which is desk-top published will look more
professional than one which is hand typed.

C6   Covering letter

Issue an explanatory letter with each questionnaire stating
clearly:

*   by whom it has been issued and to whom it should
    be returned

*   its title

*   a brief explanation of the background to, and the
    objective of, the questionnaire

*   to whom it is being issued

*   any general information or guidance on completion

*   an indication of the time likely to be needed to
    complete the questionnaire

*   an appreciation of anticipated co-operation by the
    recipient.

C7 Pilot the questionnaire

Pilot the questionnaire that has been drawn up, so that faults are discovered and corrected before it is generally issued. Also do a dummy run of the analysis you propose to carry out to check finally that the questions will give the information you require. Revise the questions as necessary, or seek clarification of objectives.

C8 Useful checklist

The following is a checklist for use when producing a questionnaire:

* will the questions listed collect all the information required?

* is every question essential?

* is the mix of questions seeking fact and opinion right?

* is all the personal information really needed for analysis?

* are any questions likely to offend or be answered evasively?

* is the question sequence logical?

* are the types of question appropriate?

* are all questions simple to understand and unambiguous?

* have cushion statements (ie statement which explain the change from one subject to another) and filter statements (ie questions which enable questions that are not relevant to be skipped over) been used where necessary?

* is it reasonable to expect the respondent to answer every question?

* will the answers be easy to record?

* does the questionnaire look good?

C9 Example customer satisfaction questionnaire

The following document is an example of a small, general customer satisfaction questionnaire. It should be issued with a covering letter (see C6 above). Organizations should devise their own series of questions according to their particular objectives.

This type of questionnaire could be for completion by customer personnel in one or more branches/sections. Its objective is to gather their opinions on:

* the quality of the IT services they use (which are governed by a service level agreement) and their level of satisfaction

* the general level of satisfaction with other services used

* the quality of, and customer satisfaction with, IT Services support personnel.

C9.1 Example questionnaire

If you are responding for a group of users please indicate how many, and your relation to them (manager, peer, etc).

**Section 1
General**

1a Which IT services are currently available to you?

Please tick those on the list below that are available to you and add up to three other services that are available and important to you. Please show the order of importance of the services available to you by putting 1 against the most important, 2 against the next most important and so on.

Service name / type   Importance

Enquiry system / read only enquiries   ☐ ☐

Account management / update   ☐ ☐

etc

Other services available to you

Service name   ☐

Service name   ☐

Service name   ☐

1b Are all the IT services you receive covered by a Service Level Agreement? If not, please list those that are not covered and indicate the number of terminals with access to the service, and your general level of satisfaction with these services using the scale (1=Excellent, 5=Very poor).

Terminals   Satisfaction

☐   ☐

☐   ☐

☐   ☐

☐   ☐

☐   ☐

1c How often are existing service level agreements, covering services you receive, reviewed and updated?

				Please tick one box
☐	☐	☐	☐	
6-monthly or more frequently	6-12 monthly	Less frequently than annually	Never been reviewed	

1d Are you kept informed of:

i   planned changes to the services which you use?

				Please tick one box
☐	☐	☐	☐	
Not at all	Sometimes	Regularly	Always	

ii   the progress of changes?

				Please tick one box
☐	☐	☐	☐	
Not at all	Sometimes	Regularly	Always	

iii when they are to be implemented?

				Please tick one box
☐	☐	☐	☐	
Not at all	Sometimes	Regularly	Always	

Section 2
Service Levels

[NOTE: There are six sets of identical questions in this
section. Please complete a set for the six (or all, if less than
six are used) most important services which you use.]

Service Name: [   ]

For questions 2a to 2e, please state how satisfied you are
with the following aspects of service provision giving a
marking on a scale of 1 - 5, as follows:

1 Excellent

2 Good

3 Satisfactory

4 Poor

5 Very poor

2a The contracted hours of service. Please state
preferred hours if a mark of 4 or 5 is given.

☐

2b The availability of this service within contracted
hours. State briefly what you consider to be the major
irritants (if any) regarding downtime.

☐

2c The current level of performance. What is your level
of satisfaction with throughput rates, response times
and turnround times?

i throughput rates (ability to consistently input all
your daily transactions) ☐

ii response times at the terminal ☐

iii batch turnround time for

- an on-line submission ☐

- manual submission ☐

2d Please give your assessment of the reliability of the service, ie is it often affected by failures and incidents?

2e How do you regard the service provided for delivery of printed reports:

   i   are reports consistently delivered by the scheduled times?

   ii is the quality of print consistently to the specified standard?

2f Do you know how much your requirements for the service will grow in the next year? (Yes/No)

   If "Yes", are the requirements included in SLAs or capacity plans? (Yes/No)

The above section is then repeated up to five more times.

**Section 3
Support Personnel**

For questions 3a to 3e, 3g and 3h, please state how satisfied you are with the following aspects of customer care, giving a marking on a scale of 1 - 5 as for questions 2a to 2e.

The Help Desk

3a How helpful are Help Desk personnel? ☐

3b How competent do you think they are? ☐

3c How satisfactory are they at keeping you informed of the status of incidents? ☐

3d How well do you rate the Help Desk for consistently dealing with incidents within the times specified in the SLA? ☐

Other IT Services personnel

3e How helpful do you find customer liaison staff? ☐

3f How useful is their role to you personally?

☐ ☐ ☐ ☐ ☐ Please tick one box

Very useful   Quite useful   A little   Not at all   Don't know

3g How satisfied are you with the service you receive from the personnel who install/maintain your terminals? ☐

[NOTE: Put a cross in the box if this question is not applicable.]

3h If you have received any training from IT Services, how satisfactory was it? ☐

[NOTE: Put a cross in the box if this question is not applicable.]

**Section 4
Other aspects of
service provision**

4a System functionality. How well do the
services and applications which you
use, provide the functions that you as
a customer were and are expecting?

☐   ☐   ☐   ☐   ☐ Please tick one box

Totally   Very well   Satisfactorily   Not entirely satisfactorily   Inadequately

4b Security. Is security and privacy of your
data and of access to the IT services via
your terminal important to you?
(Yes/No)

☐

4c If your answer is "YES", are you
satisfied with the level of security
and privacy?

☐   ☐   ☐   ☐   ☐ Please tick one box

Totally   Generally   Not quite   Not at all   Don't know

4d Disaster/recovery. Do contingency
plans exist to your knowledge?
(Yes/No)

☐

**[Note: If you have answered "NO" to this question would
you please now move on to question 5a]**

4e Have you been involved in testing
disaster recovery plans? (Yes/No)

☐

**[Note: If you have answered "YES" to this question would
you please now move on to question 5a]**

4f Do you think that you should have
been involved in testing the disaster
recovery plans? (Yes/No)

☐

Section 5
General comments

5a What is your overall level of
satisfaction with IT Services?

| | | | | | Please tick one box |

Excellent   Good   Satisfactory   Poor   Very poor

5b There is space below for any brief comments you
may wish to make on any aspect of service provision
or on how you feel that IT service quality could be
improved. (Please feel free to use this space also for
any comments you may wish to make about this
questionnaire, or any of your answers.)

[If more space is required, please use another page]

If requested, would you be prepared to help
further by participating in a short interview?

Would you please complete the name and address details
below, which are only required for checking and follow-up
purposes and will be detached from the questionnaire as
soon as it is received.

Name: _____ **Title:** _____

Section: _____ **Room No:** _____

Building/Location: _____

Tel No: _____ **Date completed:** _____

- - - **THANK YOU FOR YOUR CO-OPERATION** - - -

C10 Example analyses and figures

The following tables and figures illustrate typical analyses of customers' responses.

Customer satisfaction with service availability

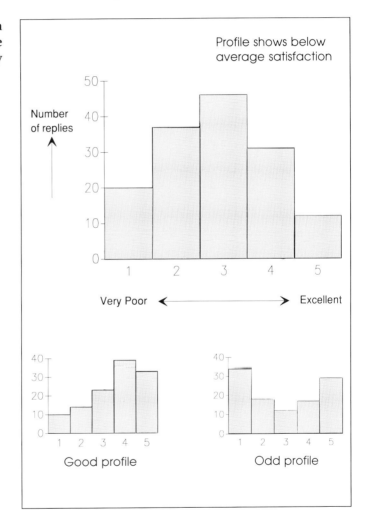

**IT Service use/
importance table**

LIST SERVICES	SLA?	No. of respondents using Service	Total no. of terminals with access	Average Importance
Service A	Y	x_1	y_1	4
Service B	N	x_2	y_2	2
Service n	..	x_n	y_n	..

Service ratings

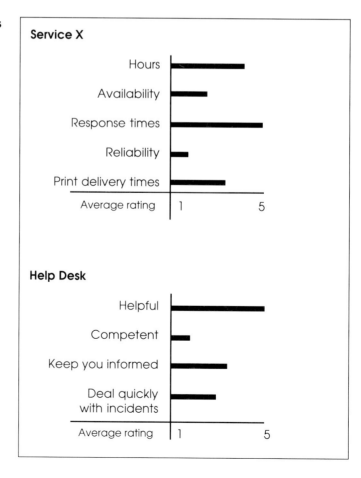

Annex D. Guidelines for professional customer contacts

The following sub-sections give guidelines on how to adopt a professional approach to contacts with customers of IT Services, covering each of the major types of contact in turn.

D1   Meetings

Meetings should:

* have an agenda drawn up and circulated in advance

* have clear objectives, known to all participants and summarized at the beginning of the meeting

* be held in an adequately-sized room with any necessary facilities available, for example an overhead projector

* have their frequency kept under review if they are held on a regular basis

* be of a relevant and acceptable length (there is nothing wrong with a meeting that lasts only 15 minutes, as long as it achieves its objectives)

* not continue for more than about 90 minutes without a break

* include only those personnel who can contribute and who need to be involved (others can be informed later)

* be properly chaired so that

    - they start on time

    - discussion does not wander from the matters in hand

    - the agenda is covered in the time available

    - all participants have a chance to contribute their views where they are relevant, and no one dominates a meeting inappropriately

    - the decisions of the meeting are clear to everyone present

    - the responsibilities for carrying out actions and their associated deadlines are agreed

    - a note is taken, to be approved at the following meeting

* have records that

    - are brief and to the point

    - specify all actions to follow the meeting, with people responsible and deadlines

    - are to a standard format, with time, date, location, subject, attendees and distribution in the heading, and have a consistent method of showing actions, date by which they must be completed, and who is responsible

    - are circulated as soon as possible after the meeting to a standard list of people including all participants, those who sent apologies, plus any others who need to be informed of progress.

D2   Phone calls

Phone calls should be:

* answered after four rings or less

* answered by giving the name of whoever answers, and the person whose phone it is, if different

* assumed to be of importance and treated as such

* answered courteously and politely, however annoying the caller is being

* followed up as agreed with the caller.

Always take the name and number of the caller, even if they say they will call back. Do not promise to pass messages on if that cannot be done, but do so quickly where possible.

D3   Letters and minutes

Correspondence should always:

* meet the organization's documentation standards

* be clear, friendly, short and to the point

* be in plain English (if you must use computer jargon explain it)

* consist of purpose, information and conclusion

* be positive and focus on the future (explain, but do not apportion blame).

Send replies to customer correspondence promptly, giving
the information requested, or explaining why it is not
available, and when it will be available.

As a final check, read through the letter or minute before it
is sent and check that it includes all the information the
recipient needs.

D4 IT Services publications

These should be well presented, whether the publication is
a report, a user manual, or a set of standards or procedures,
and should follow a pre-defined format which includes:

* agreed typeface, layout and paper, preferably
  common to the whole organization and therefore
  familiar to all

* a brief management summary and/or a synopsis so
  its content is clear at a glance

* an introduction stating the purpose, intended
  readership and scope of the document

* a conclusion and summary of recommendations, if
  appropriate

* a detachable amendment/suggestion form, if
  appropriate.

These publications should always be thoroughly proof-read
and put through a spellchecker, where available, after the
last amendments have been made before issue to customers.

D5 Electronic messages

These should be carefully controlled, and:

* be brief and to the point, but polite

* give a person to contact (and the means of contact,
  usually a phone number) in the event that the
  message is unacceptable or unclear

* explain and apologize if announcing a system shut-
  down (not 'The system will go down in 10 minutes -
  please log off now' but for example 'A fault has been
  detected in the main network processor and it is
  necessary to shut down the system for 1 hour from 12
  noon. We apologize for the inconvenience caused.')

* be used for positive messages as well as bad news

* be relevant to all recipients

* be removed as soon as they are no longer relevant.

D6 Attendance at customer site

Personal visits by IT Services staff, for example installation or maintenance staff, make a big impression on customers. These staff will be the only IT Services staff many customers meet face to face. Such staff should:

* make appointments, and keep them promptly, or phone and apologize in good time, rearranging the appointment

* complete a task at each visit, leaving an improved service behind (for example do not overlook the vital cable or part that is needed to complete a job)

* dress appropriately and be polite and helpful - do not treat customers as though they are receiving a favour when their work is probably being disrupted

* minimize the disruption they cause and clear up afterwards.

Annex E. Techniques for customer care programmes

Each customer care programme needs to be individually tailored to the IT Services organization that is carrying it out. However, information is given in this annex on six useful techniques that can be used for such programmes. (Planning a customer care programme is described in 3.1.4.2).

E1   Costs of failure

The cost of failure is one component in the overall cost of quality in an IT organization, the other two components being the cost of prevention and the cost of appraisal. The reasons for measuring the cost of failure are to:

* assess the impact on the customers' business requirements (for example, loss of competitive edge)

* provide evidence to IT management of the need for improvement

* provide a basis for monitoring and measuring success in reducing these costs and therefore overall quality costs

* identify particular problem areas.

The cost of failure can be divided into four main categories.

E1.1   Business impact

Failures which impact on the business can result in very significant costs such as:

* in a commercially run organization

    - loss of business due to customer dissatisfaction

    - loss of profits

    - financial penalties due to failure to deliver a service or product as laid down in a contract

* in a government department

    - loss of revenue due to tax demands not being despatched on time

    - the cost of resorting to a manual back-up system (if possible) for whatever time is required (hours or days)

    - inaccurate, or loss of, data for a parliamentary briefing.

E1.2 Operational

Operational cost is the cost of wasted customer time associated with:

* response times, as specified in SLAs, not being met

* service unavailability, system failures and faults.

E1.3 Rework and repair

Rework and repair costs are the time and materials costs of:

* re-running failed jobs (correction, retesting and restarting time within IT Services)

* any re-entry of data and repetition of work by users

* restoring lost data from back-ups

* reporting problems and failures, and holding meetings to discuss how to resolve problems and failures

* repairing software faults.

E1.4 Scrap

Scrap costs are those involved in having to discard materials and equipment that are no longer functioning to the required standard:

* corrupted tapes

* poor-quality paper output, incomplete or incorrect reports

* discarded software that does not meet requirements.

E1.5 Assessing failure costs

Assess failure costs by gathering information on the people-time, IT resource usage and business impact costs associated with failures, and assign these costs among the four cost categories outlined above.

Convert people-time data into costs by multiplying hours by full salary staff costs per hour. Use the organizations cost management system to convert IT resource usage to costs. Do not expect absolute accuracy - it would be prohibitively expensive to achieve. Ask a sample of customers, and all IT Services staff, to complete questionnaires, day-by-day, for two to three weeks to collect the time-based information needed.

E2   Training in customer care

Inform all IT Services staff of the implementation of a customer care programme and ensure they receive appropriate training to make them aware of its aims, objectives and implications. Provide training for IT management, technical, administrative and clerical staff. This training should take place at the launch of the programme (the start of implementation) and consist of one or two day sessions away from the workplace.

Carefully script and prepare these sessions so that they tell all staff:

*   the mission of IT Services in a comprehensible way

*   the current situation, with all its shortcomings, without making people feel defensive or inadequate

*   the improvements that are to be made, in such a way as to make everyone aware how they personally can contribute.

Make up groups of 10 to 12 with people from across the organization, including staff of all grades and from a variety of functions. In order that everyone should feel able to contribute, it is best to ask people not to mention their rank or grade but to describe their role when introducing themselves.

People need to define improvements they can make themselves, and become committed to some particular actions which will help to improve customer service. For this reason, sessions are normally participative, with group exercises, each group having a trained leader.

The logistics of organizing such sessions can be quite complex - clearly all staff cannot attend at once. A small organization may wish to have only one trained leader, and therefore plan a series of groups. Alternatively, a number of groups, each with a round table and a leader, could take place at one venue and have an overall event co-ordinator.

Senior management should show their commitment to the programme by attending such events, and describing the mission and programme themselves.

At the end of the training, participants should:

*   know and understand the organization's mission statement

* know what the customer care programme is and why it has been launched

* be committed to achieving improvements to customer service

* be aware of some actions they personally can take immediately they return to the workplace.

E3   Task forces

The setting up of task forces is referred to at stage three of planning a customer care programme (see 3.1.4.2). Task forces are set up to examine policies, practices and problems, the investigation of which has been agreed as a component part of the programme by the Steering Group.

Task forces are normally cross-functional, involving people from different parts of IT Services or the IT Directorate. The task forces report their findings and recommendations for change back to the Steering Group.

The role of a task force is often complex, and members must work closely with people they may not know well to find a solution that truly leads to improved customer service, without leading to other problems for any part of IT Services.

E4   Quality circles

A quality circle is a voluntary meeting of a peer group of staff who share a common interest in a work process and meet to identify, analyze and resolve problems which affect their performance in the workplace. Quality circles tap people's latent creativity and involve them in the implementation of improvements.

Use quality circles with care, and do not encourage them until the later stages of implementation of a customer care programme, when task forces have reported back and organization-wide changes have been made. Otherwise members of quality circles can become disillusioned by seeing major unresolved problems which management have not tackled.

Quality circles can be effective only in an environment which enables actions to be taken as a result of suggestions made.

E5 Suggestion schemes

Suggestion schemes have a chequered history, and many result in little change taking place.

For a suggestion scheme to be effective, it must be seen by staff that management seriously consider suggestions, are prepared to act on some of them and do so within a reasonable time. Encourage suggestions for improvements within a workgroup, and give managers the authority to implement them almost immediately if the group feels them to be beneficial. It should be borne in mind, however, that proposed changes may have to be submitted for change management approval.

Suggestion schemes may continue after the customer care programme is completed.

E6 Visible performance data

A key factor in raising awareness of customer service and maintaining attention is to make performance and achievement data visible to IT Services staff. Consider using posters and notices to show performance figures and record achievements - success should not be buried in a report. Photographs of award ceremonies for improvements made can be widely displayed around the computer centre.

Annex F. Example - Terms of reference for a customer liaison function

F1 Overall objective

To ensure that by effective liaison, IT Services provides its customers with the support necessary to enable them to use IT services effectively and efficiently, whilst making the most efficient use of IT resources.

F2 Specific items

1. Provide quality support to all customers of IT Services by:

   * advising and assisting IT customers to make best use of IT services and jointly determining (in line with strategies and plans) future uses to help customers derive maximum benefit

   * ensuring that IT providers are aware of customers' views and bear them in mind during the planning and provision of services.

2. Ensure customer complaints are followed-up promptly and encourage customers to participate in achieving ongoing improvement in the services provided to them.

3. Ensure that standard procedures and good practices are used in all contracts between IT Services and its customers.

4. Regularly monitor the user perception of the IT service offered and the level of user satisfaction and instigate improvements to tackle deficiencies.

5. Set up means of improving service to and relationships with customers by:

   * appointing task teams to attend to specific problems

   * encouraging 'customer groups'

   * improving communications.

6. Seek to bring about greater awareness amongst IT Services staff of the need to achieve and maintain quality customer service by different methods of communication and training.

7. Initiate projects, as agreed by IT management, aimed at ensuring overall improvements in IT/customer relationships (for example a customer care programme).

IT Infrastructure Library
Customer Liaison

Comments Sheet

CCTA hopes that you find this book both useful and interesting. We will welcome your comments and suggestions for improving it.
Please use this form or a photocopy, and continue on a further sheet if needed.

From: re: 1990/CL

              Name

      Organization

          Address

        Telephone

COVERAGE
Does the material cover your needs?
If not, then what additional material would you like included.

CLARITY
Are there any points which are unclear?
If yes, please detail where and why.

ACCURACY
Please give details of any inaccuracies found.

If more space is required for these or other comments, please continue overleaf.

IT Infrastructure Library
Customer Liaison

OTHER COMMENTS

Return to: **IT Infrastructure Management Services**
              CCTA
              Gildengate House
              Upper Green Lane
              NORWICH, NR3 1DW

Further information

Further information on the contents of this module can be obtained from:

IT Infrastructure Management Services
CCTA
Gildengate House
Upper Green Lane
NORWICH
NR3 1DW

Telephone 0603 694808
(GTN 3014 - 4808).

The price of this publication has been set to make a contribution to the costs incurred by CCTA in preparing the copy.

Printed in the United Kingdom for HMSO
Dd293180 11/90 C12